SMALL TOWN AND RURAL POLICE

SMALL TOWN AND RURAL POLICE

By

VICTOR H. SIMS, Ph.D.

Assistant Professor of Criminal Justice
Department of Sociology, Social Work, and Criminal Justice
Lamar University
Beaumont, Texas

A GIFT from
TSU
Ft. Benning, GA

CHARLES C THOMAS • PUBLISHER
Springfield • Illinois • U.S.A.

Published and Distributed Throughout the World by
CHARLES C THOMAS • PUBLISHER
2600 South First Street
Springfield, Illinois 62794-9265

© *1988 by* CHARLES C THOMAS • PUBLISHER
ISBN 0-398-05405-3
Library of Congress Catalog Card Number: 87-23280

With THOMAS BOOKS *careful attention is given to all details of manufacturing and design. It is the Publisher's desire to present books that are satisfactory as to their physical qualities and artistic possibilities and appropriate for their particular use.* THOMAS BOOKS *will be true to those laws of quality that assure a good name and good will.*

Printed in the United States of America
Q-R-3

Library of Congress Cataloging in Publication Data

Sims, Victor H.
    Small town and rural police / by Victor H. Sims.
       p. cm.
    Bibliography: p.
    Includes index.
    ISBN 0-398-05405-3
    1. Police, Rural--United States. 2. Police--United States.
I. Title.
HV7965.S56 1988   87-23280
363.2'0973--dc19   CIP

DEDICATION

MORE variance occurs among police departments and policing methods and procedures than among police officers themselves. This book is dedicated to all street police officers, current and former, who have enjoyed policing. I've known officers who suffered every misery and tragedy life has to offer. Yet, every officer I've known, without exception, took great pride and found endless entertainment in recalling the comedy, the absurd, the ridiculous, and always the unexpected, and the good times and good friends of their police experiences.

This book is also dedicated to the other members of my favorite small group, Cookie, Jim, Bob, and Glenda.

CONTENTS

SMALL TOWN AND RURAL POLICE

Part I

INTRODUCTION AND DEFINITIONS

Chapter 1

INTRODUCTION

S MALL TOWN and rural police remain the quintessence of policing.

Scholarly study of small town and rural police generates greater hope and promise for future improvement of policing than does any other field of inquiry. Small town and rural police routinely demonstrate numerous methods, concepts, attitudes, and a philosophy which appear fundamental to effective policing. Recent research in this subject yields valuable lessons and suggestions for increasing police effectiveness. Ideas gained from observing small town and rural police point the way to futuristic policing for all police departments, regardless of size.

Personal interaction between police and citizens, an encompassing community spirit of caring, informality, community-based policing, and a police philosophy of matching service to community expectations contribute to the uniqueness, success, and effectiveness of small town and rural police. With these trademark characteristics and unencumbered with bureaucratic requirements, small town and rural police work toward human goals of helping people police themselves.

Small town and rural police remained ignored, criticized, vilified, stereotyped, and ridiculed for more than a century in the United States. The common image of the small town or rural police officer equates with that of a stumbling, incompetent buffoon who enjoys an unusually good day if he survives without hospitalization or incarceration. Often pictured as a complete clown and the brunt of most humor in town, he knows absolutely nothing about modern policing and practices little or no law enforcement.

Popular television shows portray the police officer in the big city as a dynamic superman—able to solve and resolve any problem, crime, or police situation anywhere, any time, in a few minutes. He never stumbles, falls, displays poor judgement, or makes an improper deci-sion. He seems the perfect boy scout even though forced to ignore another's constitutional rights occasionally. This does not bother him be-cause he believes that when one acts in the interest of justice the ends al-ways justify the means.

In contrast, the small town or rural police officer seems portrayed quite opposite with no explanation as to why. Pictured as a moron and a lazy misfit, he seems corrupt, immoral, and totally without professional ethics. The criminals appear as good guys in a perverted role reversal leaving the small town or rural police officer easily recognizable as the problem source. The viewer receives reinforcement to believe the de-viant citizen represents justice and the small town or rural police officer its jocular antithesis.

This poor image of small town and rural police began more than 100 years ago and relates to the public's view of itself in general and po-licing in particular. After uniformed municipal police departments were formed in the larger cities of the North and East prior to the Civil War, cor-ruption soon followed. Most large city police departments started with only a few officers and increased their numbers over the years. Numerous factors contributed to the corruption including lack of leadership, absence of any training, corruption of big city governments, acceptance of police corrup-tion by the public, and a ward system of government. Police training did not exist at that time, and its only close resemblance seemed the uniformity of practices in the larger police departments. Small town and rural police lacked such uniformity because of rapid personnel turnover, no interagency communication, and a trial-and-error approach to policing. Therefore, small town and rural police practices were perceived as different, back-ward, and inappropriate, even though these practices remained no more il-legal or corrupt than the practices of the police in big cities.

After the Civil War, policing in the South appeared marginal at best and frequently nonexistent. Carpetbaggers and scalawags moved into city governments throughout the South and reconstruction costs grew at an immeasurable pace. Some of the larger cities experienced federal troops serving as police for years afterwards. In the pre-Civil War South, slaves received blame for most crime. The war ended but racism did not. After the war people believed the new liberated status of blacks explained crime which was otherwise unresolved. The police mirrored the feelings and attitudes of their communities with racism in the South and corruption in the Northeast. Every police department remains a child of its parent city, large or small.

The West seemed no exception. Westerners have always taken pride in their frontier pioneer spirit. They did not take crime or criminals lightly, and a rough and reckless code of the West emerged in their early justice and police system. Many enjoy the stories and tall tales of Judge Roy Bean's justice and his law west of the Pecos, while very few realize Judge Bean dispensed justice as an elected and reelected magistrate who satisfied the needs and demands of his constituency. The West produced numerous small town and rural police officers and police departments with notorious reputations, both good and bad.

Universally, police always dealt with problems of theft, assault, violence, and murder. It seems, therefore, a short step to understanding how the police might at times resort to apparently easy and quick, albeit illegal and unethical, methods to solve such problems. It takes a thief to catch a thief; exactly this happened in the West. Police responded to violence with violence. Lawless police practices seemed not totally out of place in a lawless community. The evolution of policing in the West remained essentially no different than its counterparts in the South and Northeast. The police echoed the feelings and attitudes of their communities with quick decisive action and homemade, sometimes violent, justice. As outlaw Bob Younger observed in Stillwater prison, "We were rough men playing a rough game."

The mayor, city manager, city council form of government in the West helps explain the relative absence of police corruption, but the certain and severe police delivery of curbstone justice remains explained only by the western frontier pioneer spirit. In the western-most point of the old west, Nome, Alaska, Rex Beach wrote, "There is no law of God nor man, north of fifty three."

During the first half of the 20th century, U.S. policing began to improve. Berkeley, California, Police Chief, August Vollmer, did more to improve policing in the United States than any other person before or since. The existence of a university bearing his name in Santa Ana, California gives powerful testimony to his vision, insight, and influence. His inspirational leadership in the police world remains unforgotten. As an exemplary street officer, police chief, university professor, and internationally recognized police authority, he introduced dozens of profound concepts to the police community. These included community-based policing, community service, police education, the application of management and organization principles to police administration, crime prevention, advanced communications, and the application of the scientific method to police science.

There seems little doubt, however, that Vollmer's major contributions to the evolution of policing remain his teachings of modern administration, scientific detection, community-based policing, and continuous education and training of officers. His police philosophy was so profound and his leadership so inspiring that decades after his death Berkeley police experience continues to be viewed as a graduate school in a police career development. The Berkeley Police Department has produced literally scores of police chiefs, administrators, sheriffs, and educators practicing and teaching the Vollmer philosophy throughout the world. For decades, no police department came close to producing as many chiefs as the Berkeley Police Department, although now the Lakewood, Colorado Police Department seriously challenges this record.

The University of California at Berkeley claims to graduate more people with a bachelor's degree who subsequently earn a Ph.D. than any other single campus in the United States. Likewise, the Berkeley Police Department claims more former officers who went on to earn a doctorate than any other police department can claim. All of this indicates the enormous influence Vollmer exerted on modern policing.

Chief Vollmer began his famous police career in 1905 in Berkeley with only four officers. Although he made tremendous contributions over the next half century, like so many visionaries, he remained so far ahead of his time that followers would not fully understand and appreciate his works until years after his death. The few police departments following Vollmer's teachings seemed mostly larger agencies with more resources and less to risk with experimentation. Small town and rural police departments remained too involved in day-to-day survival and usually employed no one possessing much interest in the latest police thinking. The great depression of the early thirties also contributed to police improvement by providing a pool of highly qualified people eager to work.

During the years from WWI to WWII the crack between big city and small town policing rapidly widened. The population movement from rural areas to urban centers accelerated, and we became a mobile society. Many successful criminals of that era owed their continued freedom to two things: the automobile and unsophisticated small town and rural police. The automobile transported the criminal quickly away from the crime and frequently into the rural countryside or suburbs. There the police either did not know that person as a criminal or did not want to disrupt the tranquil status quo. Larger police departments possessed the budgets necessary for improved police communications, criminal investigation, and police equipment. Even as late as the sixties and seventies, when many assumed that all police cars had police radios and reliable communications, many small town and rural police departments could claim no radio communications. Telephones provided the only remote contact.

During the nineteenth century, with policing evolving and maturing, small town and rural police strategies and concepts were unconsciously applied to larger police departments with virtually no success. Many police departments held on to traditions as they expanded from three or four officers to several hundred, but small town and rural police solutions did not work with big city problems. Now in the last quarter of the twentieth century police administrators apply big city police solutions to small town and rural police problems with the same results — total failure.

The factual basis for the undesirable reputation of small town and rural police began during prohibition and the great depression, solidified during the forties and fifties, reached its zenith with the civil rights movement, and ended rather abruptly in the late sixties and early seventies with the birth of the Law Enforcement Assistance Administration (LEAA) and state-mandated police standards. The civil rights movement put small town and rural police in the South on television's evening news. The American public refused to tolerate such police activity, forcing small town and rural police to clean up their act. As people change, their police change, but not before. Seven or eight landmark U.S. Supreme Court decisions involving search and seizure, defendants' rights, and police tactics during the sixties also drastically altered traditional policing. These cases mandated such radical departure from customary policing that many career officers could not adapt to the new methods and subsequently departed police work.

LEAA began operations in the late sixties and immediately started pouring billions of dollars into the criminal justice system. Few today will debate that the police did not receive the lion's share. A disproportionate lesser amount of that police money eventually trickled down to small town and rural police, but their major benefit from the LEAA era remained intangible. As a direct result of LEAA and numerous blue ribbon committees, almost every state established a commission to set and oversee compliance with minimum hiring, education, and training standards for police. Confusing matters, each state referred to their commission or board or office by a different title. Small town and rural police now perceived goals and expectations the same as other police.

In May, 1984, the Mt. Dora, Florida, Police Department, with only seventeen officers, was identified as an exemplary organization when it became the first police agency to achieve accreditation by The Commission on Accreditation for Law Enforcement Agencies, Inc. In 1979 The National Sheriffs' Association, The Police Executive Research Forum, The National Organization of Black Law Enforcement Executives, and The International Association of Chiefs of Police worked together and established The Commission on Accreditation for Law Enforcement Agencies, Inc. This commission exists as an independent, nonprofit organization, directed by a 21-member board with a goal of developing universal applicable police standards. Standards appear the first step toward improving police. Mt. Dora Police Department's accreditation remains an honor for them and suggests the coming of age of small town and rural police.

Any remaining evidence supporting the ugly reputation of small town and rural police evaporated under the heat of LEAA and the states' police standards bodies. However, like other bad reputations, the one small town and rural police acquired proved difficult to dismiss. This unfortunate image continued through the seventies and eighties and flourishes today with no end in sight. But a stereotype can outlive its usefulness. This book attempts to show the incompetent and ineffective image of small town and rural police now appears undeserved and inaccurate. Public perceptions of small town and rural police seem inconsistent with reality.

Patrick Donovan's dissertation in 1970 appears to be the first major research investigating how different size police departments vary. Donovan and others note that researchers and serious students of the police completely ignore small town and rural police. A review of the literature on small town and rural police for my master's thesis in 1975 and my doctoral dissertation in 1982 found no significant new additions. Small town and rural police remain the great unexplored mystery of the criminal justice system.

The 14,000 member International Association of Chiefs of Police, with a polished monthly magazine, *The Police Chief,* seems the largest and most professional organization of its kind in the world. It contributes significantly to improving policing with research and training. One of its standing committees concerns small police departments. Incongruously, the chief of a police department with 90 police employees chaired the IACP's 1984 Small Police Department Committee. With 90 percent of the 21,000 police departments in the United States employing *fewer* than ten officers each, it certainly seems somewhat inappropriate for the chief of a 90-officer police department to chair the Small Police Department Committee. When this committee met during the IACP's annual conference in 1984, the guest speaker, a university professor, presented the results of a study concerning the investigative function of police departments with ten or *more* officers.

The majority of police departments remained snubbed. Since the vast majority of United States police chiefs command police departments with ten or fewer officers, it seems reasonable to expect a police chief's association to focus on those. This appears more than a casual or coincidential ignoring of small town and rural police departments. These common attitudes possessed by some police, social scientists, the general public, and mass communications seem best summarized in *The Police Chief* statement, "A department with less than ten must call upon divine help. . . . " (1974). Social researchers and students of policing must confront reality and rely on scientific methods; they must leave the issue of divine guidance to the police chaplains, and study all police departments regardless of size if they expect their findings to accurately describe police of the United States. Scholarly police research requires nothing less.

A closer and more rigorous investigation and study of small town and rural police reveal some surprising and even astonishing conclusions. Differences between small city and big city policing definitely exist, but the differences and similarities appear far from what the popular image magnifies and totally opposite to what many believe.

An empirical comparison of police departments by the number of officers each employs exposes evidence contradicting long-held beliefs; seriously challenges major themes, attitudes, and philosophies of policing; and explodes many myths about small town and rural police.

In 1973 Auten wrote:

> If the advancement of law enforcement toward the elusive goal of professionalization is to continue, then all law enforcement organizations must be improved. To neglect the smaller law enforcement agency is to care for the exposed portion of the plant while neglecting the roots. These smaller law enforcement organizations form the backbone of law enforcement in this country and in the end will be the yardstick against which our efforts toward professionalization will be measured. (p. viii)

I agree with Auten's recognition that all sizes of police departments need improvement. But simply because small town and rural police seem neglected in the past does not mean they must change more than larger police departments to improve policing in the United States. Change does not always result in improvement. Based on my experiences as a police officer and chief working with both urban and rural police departments, large and small, and based on study and research, I remain convinced beyond a reasonable doubt that in many ways small town and rural police provide a model for future policing in the United States.

The concept of community-oriented policing (cop) adopted by several large police departments and studied by the Police Foundation appears to be no newer than August Vollmer. For many decades small town and rural police lived and worked *community-based policing,* and they will continue to do so. Community-oriented policing and community-based policing are simply one and the same. This seems reminiscent of the musician who played a piano in a house of prostitution for twenty years before learning the shocking news of what happened upstairs. It remains the nature of the beast in a large bureaucracy to reinvent the wheel. Some ancient truths seem indisputable and unavoidable. So it remains with policing.

The relationship usually found between the small town or rural officer and an individual citizen seems absolutely essential for continual, effective policing regardless of the size of the police department or the chemistry of the community. The police chief of the big city offering a multitude of reasons, excuses, and thinly veiled apologies to explain why his officers do not cultivate such personal relationships has avoided the important fact that this omission is the very reason his agency's effectiveness remains low. He fools no one but the most gullible into believing that effective policing exists without this personal interaction.

Policing is community involvement or it is nothing. It always has been and it always will be. Police technology changes almost daily to help make the street officer's job easier. The law and policy which the street officer must know and understand changes almost weekly. But perhaps more important than all this, one thing about policing that never changes remains the relationship between one officer and one person, suspect, victim, witness, drunk, informant, juvenile, chronic complainer, thief, or curious know-nothing bystander. This relationship will always exist. The more personal interaction involved in this relationship then the greater the probability that the officer will obtain his goals — which means more effective policing.

Personal interaction occurs in two arenas in small town and rural policing. It occurs between the individual officer and every other officer on that particular police department, and it also is found between a police officer on that police department and individual citizens in the community. This does not happen because the officer belongs to two groups—the police department and the community—but because the two groups appear more integrated as one than segregated as two. The small town or rural police department remains, to use Dr. Radelet's tired but powerful cliche, *a part of* the community and not *apart from* the community. This personal interaction seems in practice more of a philosophy of policing than a method of policing. This is not to say that positive interpersonal relationships are not found in some larger police departments such as Houston, San Diego, or Newark; but rather this phenomena seems to occur with greater frequency in small town and rural police departments.

This high degree of personal interaction so common in small town and rural policing remains the key to understanding the major differences between small and big town police. Investigating and better understanding of these differences remain the goal of this book.

Chapter 2

HOW SMALL IS SMALL?

ANY SCHOLARLY study of small town and rural police must begin with a definition of terms. This remains necessary since no typology of police departments by size exists. Therefore no common definition of small town and rural police exists.

Police agencies seem sized in numerous ways by the mass media, writers and authorities on police subjects. Definitions of police department sizes seem best described according to the orientation of their authors. However, almost all of these descriptions fit neatly into one of three categories: first, by the number of police officers employed; second, by the population of the jurisdiction; and third, by the degree of social interaction present.

The first method of defining police department size with a hard definition contains obvious advantages: accuracy, convenience, and simplicity. Unfortunately, however, numerous hidden disadvantages surface when applying definition by number such as inaccurate generalizing, stereotyping, and labeling. The most in-depth and extensive study ever undertaken of United States police resulted in the 1973 publication of a large volume, entitled *Report on Police* by the National Advisory Commission on Criminal Justice Standards and Goals. It defined police department size by the number of officers.

The National Advisory Commission divided police departments into six categories according to the number of police officers employed: 1 to 15, 16 to 75, 76 to 150, 151 to 400, 401 to 1,000, and more than 1,000. Such grouping is not as arbitrary as might first appear, because this sizing also suggests the degree of specialization and decentralization present. Police departments at one end of the spectrum, those with fifteen or fewer officers, usually employ generalists, seem totally centralized, and possess little or no specialization. The four categories between the two

15

extremes claim varying degrees of specialization and decentralization. The National Advisory Commission made no attempt to label their six categories and that proved regrettable. Students and writers groped in the dark for a size label to stick on a police department. I have labeled and defined the most frequent appearing police department size, those with fifteen or fewer officers, as small town and rural police departments.

Most writers referring to a police department as small or large never define their terms. In one article, when defining the size of small police departments, the authors labeled a police department with ten or fewer officers as "micro" and police departments with fifteen to thirty officers as "small." They fail to mention police departments with eleven to four-teen officers. Perhaps these would be micro-small. "Micro" hardly seems appropriate when many dictionaries define "micro" as abnormally small. Police departments with fewer than eleven officers remain many things, but they are not abnormal; conversely, they are the norm.

Some police scholars contend that 90 percent of the nation's 40,000 police departments each employ fewer than ten officers. Others pro-claim that 90 percent of the United States' 17,000 police departments can claim fewer than ten officers each. The difference of opinion clearly concerns how many police departments exist in the United States, rather than the disproportionately large percentage of police depart-ments with fewer than ten officers. The fact that the majority of police departments employ fewer than ten officers per agency remains undis-puted. Add to this the fact that more than 80 percent of police de-partments employ fewer than five officers per agency and it seems undeniable that small town and rural police departments do not appear abnormal because of their size.

Ambiguously, one writer labels as small those police departments with 15 to 75 officers each, while another considers a police department with 100 officers small. A LEAA study stereotyped small police depart-ments as those with fewer than 25 officers each. Apparently those LEAA writers were unfamiliar with the National Advisory Commission's *Report on Police* since two different definitions were used: *Report on Police* did not use 25 as a cut-off point. Even the offices of the federal government can-not agree on one definition of a small police department. Until now, all writers encountered difficulty in describing smaller police departments, because no common language existed. Accuracy appears a major advan-tage of a number classification scheme. A police department with 500 officers remains precisely fifty times greater than a police department with ten.

Similarly, the temptation to reduce ratio data to nominal categories proves probably the major disadvantage of this method of defining police departments by size. Too frequently, students and writers reduce this ratio data to nominal data and group police departments into categories. Pigeon-holing police departments into two, rural and urban, three, small, medium-sized, and large, or six neat groups assists the researcher or writer. These quantified commonalities permit easy grouping of police departments by size, but unfortunately this leads to over generalizing. The lure to convert continuous data to categorical data seems irresistible to many and frequently results in false generalities. While labeling by the number of officers provides a convenient handle to grasp the subject, it also results in negative stereotyping. Virtually everyone who reads current events or watches television witnesses such stereotyping of small town and rural police by the mediacracy.

Labeling and stereotyping seem dangerous when considering many different police departments, because often such consideration results in false statements and glaring misconceptions. The categories are established in terms of one variable, the number of officers on a police department, and then conclusions drawn about totally different variables, such as training. For instance, the popular image of small town and rural police concludes that they possess less training than do their big city counterparts. This is a fallacy. In this particular example of stereotyping and generalizing, the conclusion remains false. Empirical studies presented later in this book find no significant relationship between officers' average training time and police department size.

Likewise, the measurement criterion itself seems flawed and prejudiced. It assumes that the greater number of officers a police department employs, then the more the police department will possess of other characteristics: the larger a police department, then the more decentralization, the more employees, and bigger budget it will claim. The innuendo appears unavoidable—the bigger the better. Unfortunately, the measurement criterion used in the largest police study ever conducted makes no mention of the numerous desirable factors more frequently found in small town and rural policing and less frequently found in big city and megaplex policing.

Advantages of this first category of ways of defining police department size include accuracy and convenience. Classifying police departments by the number of officers employed remains easy and precise, and it provides the researcher with ratio data. A police department with 1,000 officers is exactly twice as large as one with 500 officers and 100 times larger than a police department with ten officers. Likewise, a police department that loses all its officers provides the true zero needed for ratio data. Very few would attempt to argue, however, that a police department with 1,000 officers polices 100 times more efficiently or effectively than does the police department with 10 officers. A haunting possibility remains that the smaller police department can police more effectively than can the larger one. The most glaring disadvantage of this category of definitions appears that it too often results in false generalities, inappropriate hypothetical grouping, incorrect labeling and undeserved stereotyping.

The second category of size definitions for police departments involves grouping according to the number or nature of a jurisdiction's population. Most such attempts seem based on census reports. These definitions often incorrectly assume that two towns with approximately the same population will maintain police departments of comparable sizes. The Federal Bureau of Investigation's annual *Uniform Crime Reports* uses this method in some of its analyses. Jurisdictions within a certain population range are grouped together and assumed to support police departments of approximately the same size.

Again, convenience seems the major advantage. A statistician possesses the population data but not the number of officers on certain police departments. In this category the number of police employees does not matter. The jurisdiction's population remains easily determined from census data and inferences are then made that service areas in the same population range will retain police departments of similar sizes. Frequently, great disparity appears in the number of officers employed by towns of almost identical sizes. The fact that some jurisdictions experience a tenfold seasonal population increase with no corresponding fluctation in police department strength compounds the problem.

Sometimes the disparity seems best explained by the social nature of the communities. For example, a bedroom community with 18,000 people bores its eight police officers. In contrast, the nearby industrial town of 18,000 includes two sawmills, hundreds of oilfield workers, eighteen bars, and sixteen overworked police officers. Two towns exhibit the same population, but one's police department remains twice as great as the other's. Such examples seem common. They produce frustration when a survey groups a commuter community with twenty officers having nothing to do but check vacation homes and generate meaningless busy work, together with a boomtown community with twenty officers who often respond to barroom fights wearing pajamas showing beneath police jackets. Often the latter of the two departments initiate paperwork primarily on certain felonies, making statistics concerning workload completely misleading or at best ambiguous.

Economics frequently explain the different sizes of police departments. For example, two sister cities exist of approximately the same population. The first claims much industry and a greater tax base. Citizens of the second enjoy clean air with no polluting industries and an almost tax-free economy. Although the two remain the same size, in square miles and population, the first maintains three times as many officers as does the second. Consequently, grouping these two police departments together clearly violates basic assumptions. Often statisticians group police departments in this manner but fail to mention crime rates or workloads.

The chief advantage of grouping police departments by the number of people in the service area remains convenience since the data appears readily available. A crucial disadvantage is that such an approach includes a fatal error: the assumption that cities within the same population range will maintain police departments of similar sizes. This assumption proves false too often to seem useful. Although many chiefs try, few municipal governments are financially willing to employ police officers to match a preset ratio of officers per 1,000 citizens.

At other times the variance in the number of police officers employed by towns of comparable size remains mostly unexplained, and the reasons for the disparity between police department sizes escapes identification.

Examining the population of a jurisdiction also involves a look at the social nature of the group and is, perhaps, the most difficult. Few venture to examine the chemistry of the populace in the terms of police department size. *Exurbs* appear as urban islands in rural settings, not uncommon but still causing curiosity and confusion in the labeling of police departments. Likewise, little effort seems exerted in distinguishing between surburban, urban, and rural police departments. When the social chemistry of a community excites a heavy police workload, the justification for the resulting call for more officers seems based solely on workload with no reference to the composition of the service area. Almost never does this request for increased police authorizations allude to possible expectations of proportionate increases in police effectiveness.

The social chemistry of any town suggests not only the proper size of the police department but the type of policing required. Looking at the nature of the population suggests that the sociology of the police department would ideally match the sociology of the community. Using the western boomtown as an example, boomtown workers work hard and play hard. Certain behavior and work environments correlate with increased alcohol abuse, family fights, and violence, all demanding more police officers. This boomtown phenomenon, known as the Gillette syndrome, accounts for exponential growth rates in police work-load in some energy rich towns.

Although the boomtown and the university town have disparate populations, writers continue grouping together small town police departments and university police departments because they employ about the same number of officers. Again, such grouping and resulting comparison seems subject to serious questioning. The agencies are grouped using one variable, the number of police employees, but compared using another variable, the nature of the policed populace. This seems the classic example of comparing apples and oranges.

The working environment of the police varies enormously. Too many have assumed too long that police tasks remain unchanged or vary only with the size of the police department. Social and psychological environments of policing vary greatly from city to city, even within the same population range. As the comparison of boomtown and university town populations illustrated, two cities with exactly the same population range can demonstrate totally different sociological configurations. It seems more reasonable to match the social nature of the police department to that of the community, as occurs in small town and rural policing, than attempt a forced match between the ratio of police officers to citizens with some totally meaningless average taken from dissimilar police departments in states on the other side of the continent. Accepting a false hypothesis as true is a type one error: the supposition that similar-sized towns maintain similar-sized police departments is a type one error.

Leading advantages of grouping police departments by the sociology of the community include accuracy and validity. This grouping method is seldom employed since its most outstanding disadvantage remains the extreme difficulty involved in measurement. Measuring the social environment and temperament of a community with any degree of accuracy is most difficult, requiring skilled research sociologists and great expense. It remains far easier to apply a simple ratio, such as 2.5 officers per 1,000 citizens, to a population count in order to calculate the supposedly ideal number of officers. A few researchers attempt to combine these two when drawing a rural-urban distinction.

Most attempts to distinguish between rural and urban police departments meet with little success. The U.S. Bureau of the Census explains rural as an area of open country or towns with less than a 2,500 population. This definition permits the possibility of rural areas and rural residents inside an incorporated city but limits the size to 2,500. Another definition of rural includes those areas outside a standard metropolitan statistical area. Some police departments having up to 75 or more officers serving communities up to 30,000 or more people seem very rural police departments upon close inspection.

Still many other police departments exist with fewer than five or ten officers that police a small suburb completely surrounded by a sprawling standard metropolitan statistical area with a million or more residents. These police departments remain very urban, regardless of the number of officers each employs. Traditional correlations between the number of officers on a police department and its description as rural or urban seem to have crumbled in recent years. The rural officer still exists, but it is increasingly difficult to distinguish between rural police and small town police.

The Rural Sociological Society has struggled for a suitable definition of rural for over fifty years without satisfactory results. Perhaps rurality exists more as a state of mind and attitude than as an area on a map or a ratio of persons per square mile. Rurality may be best defined subjectively.

A few researchers and writers refuse to release the past and insist that rural means only that area far from civilization where major police problems include snakebites, lost livestock, and loneliness. A tired thirty-year veteran street officer once remarked, "I love police work. It's all those damned people I can't tolerate."

Others attempt to separate metropolitan and nonmetropolitan policing. The term metropolitan means urban city and surburban areas while the term nonmetropolitan means small town and rural. The rural-urban distinction sometimes appears equivalent to nonmetropolitan and metropolitan. A stronger case seems possible that rural-urban differences should not be viewed as nomative data but should be considered as a continuum. Rurality appears as a matter of degree and not in absolute categories. Thus, one town, even though larger, might appear more rural than another.

If the social chemistry of the populace of a jurisdiction seems more appropriate in defining the size of a police department, then certainly the infinite number of possibilities would be correctly addressed with a measure of infinite degrees and ratio data rather than a measure of a few categories and nominal data.

From a small town and rural police viewpoint, the first two categories of definitions of police department sizes appear negative. They both imply or state that small town and rural police departments lack something which other police departments possess because of their greater size. The third and last category for definitions of police departments by size involves the social interaction between individual officers or, as will be explained later in the book, between the police officers and the community. All the definitions in this third category suggest that the small town and rural police possess some qualities which larger police departments lack. From the vantage point of effective policing this last category seems positive.

Just as many definitions exist for the small town or rural police department as exist for other small groups. However, the most durable and bulletproof definition of small town and rural police involves the notion of direct, face-to-face interaction. In small town and rural police departments, every member personally knows and directly interacts with every other member; and each officer repeatedly engages many community members in social interaction. Initially, the small town or rural police department is best defined not in absolute numbers but by the presence of personal, direct, intimate, and informal interaction occurring regularly among all group members. This personal and informal social interaction among all group members remains a uniqueness of small town and rural police.

The face-to-face interaction between each officer and every other member of the police department and between each officer and a relatively high percentage of community members remains an exclusive hallmark asset of small town and rural police. Larger police departments do not and cannot practice this desirable quality. Direct and intimate communication and social intercourse so desirable in policing seem prohibited by the size and nature of large bureaucratic police departments. These characteristics exist as the rule on small town and rural police departments and as the exception on big city police departments. These personal, informal, intimate, and direct interaction attributes remain the same qualities which contribute to improved police community relations and effective policing sought by all police departments, regardless of size.

Several phenomena occur in the small town or rural police setting, resulting from group size and contributing to more effective policing. Social interaction exists as one such phenomenon, and psychological group formation exists as another. The latter develops from the former.

Psychologists refer to certain small groups as psychological groups while sociologists call them primary groups. The two terms, psychological group and primary group, as used in this context, seem interchangable.

A psychological group cannot exist without direct, face-to-face interaction. Members of a psychological group share common objectives, they identify with the group, and their needs are satisfied as a direct result of belonging to that group. Psychological group members experience strong emotional attachment to their group. They confide and share with each other on a personal level which never appears in a larger group. Members of small town and rural police departments possess the same goals and needs as anyone else, but their goals seem obtained and their needs fulfilled because they belong to small town and rural police groups. Officers working for a larger police department share similar goals and needs, but such goals and needs remain unobtained and unfulfilled by the police department because its size and bureaucratic practices make psychological group formation impossible.

Any police department exists as a physical group—a collection of individuals, but only those police departments with relatively few officers cultivate and nourish psychological group formation. At some point the police department simply becomes too large for psychological group formation. Most authorities on small groups agree on twenty as the absolute upper limit for a small group and fifteen as the usual upper limit. A police department with more than twenty members lacks the face-to-face interaction between all officers. Close examination of psychological groups reveals they almost never include more than fifteen members.

The reason for this seems surprisingly simple. Our socialization process prepares us, on the average, to deal with up to seven others on the job in a face-to-face informal way. The average person cannot psychologically handle more than seven in the working environment. This number changes in other cultures, but in our culture it remains at a maximum of seven. More than seven tends to make the average person feel overwhelmed with too many personalities and too many relationships. A small group with fifteen members contains a total of 105 possible different one-to-one relationships. Appendix A illustrates this with fifteen circles joined by 105 lines. Some individuals in this group might interact with only one or two others, and some might interact with all fourteen others, but the average person will interact with seven others (105 divided by fifteen equals seven). When group size increases from fifteen to sixteen more happens than the mere obvious. A group of six-teen forces members to deal with an average of 7.5 one-on-one encoun-ters. This proves too much for the average U.S. citizen.

Therefore, psychological groups seem almost always limited to fif-teen or fewer members. In a group of fifteen or fewer, the average mem-ber might not like everyone else, but each member believes he knows every other member well. In a group of sixteen or more, the average member believes that one or two other group members seem not known well enough to be trusted; or one is considered a stranger or outsider. The psychological group with more than fifteen members appears only as a rare exception.

Even the United States President belongs to a small group of close confidants. This group may include congressmen, cronies, Cabinet Sec-retaries, White House staffers, or outsiders who claim no other obvious connection to the Washington political scene. This small group of behind-the-scenes power players significantly influence those who run the country. A small group of senior, battle-scarred Congressmen serve in key positions or chair key committees, chair subcommittees, and ger-rymander bills or permit them to die in committee. Sometimes this group, in effect, controls the more than 500-member Congress and or-chestrates the legislative branch of government. The third branch re-mains dominated by a small group of nine, and a smaller included group of five to eight frequently decide law.

Football teams include several strings and separate offense and de-fense units. The road team might include thirty members but at any one time only eleven players play ball. Ideally, all eleven belong to the same psychological group. One player would be a member of the football team, a physical group of 45; the road team, a social group of thirty; and also a member of the starting offensive unit, which plays as a psychologi-cal group of eleven, if the coach is effective.

Police remain a very close knit, clannish fraternity. The hurdles faced by minorities and women trying to enter police careers consist more of group entrance requirements than of racist or sexist prejudices. When the police applicant is hired, that person becomes a member of a physi-cal group, the police department. When that same person completes the initial training and begins to work the streets as a uniformed police officer, he will most likely be accepted by fellow officers and become a member of a social group. If the individual does not fit into the group and the group rejects him as a member, then the social group, especially small town and rural police departments, will tend to ostracize that individual. Police officers ostracize fellow officers, because their behavior does not fit into expected police behavior patterns, not because of the race, sex, or ethnic identification of the outcast.

Yet another criterion remains for individuals on small town and rural police departments. Not only must the social group accept the new officer, but the psychological group must accept the officer also. Second only to the relationship between partners, primary group ties remain the strongest bonds possible in the police world. Many examples exist of a strong, determined individual surviving through years of social ostracism on a larger police department. For an officer to endure even a few months of primary group ostracism in small town and rural police departments remains almost unknown. Primary group acceptance is one of our strongest, inherent social needs.

Most career officers experience the special bonding between partners. The small town or rural officer additionally experiences feelings of loyal attachment to his police department because the police department and the psychological group remain one and the same. The work group is the primary group.

Psychological groups may exist on larger police departments, although the size of the group itself usually does not exceed fifteen and never more than twenty. The police department itself in such a situation remains no part of the psychological group. In a small town or rural police department, the police department itself satisfies the needs and goals of the individual. The officer so fortunate as to belong to a psychological group in a big city police department finds his need to feel worthwhile met by that group and not by the police department. Consequently the officer knows loyalty only to that small group, not the police department or the city.

The officer on the big city police department who belongs to a psychological group feels and expresses linkages only to that group, not to the employing police department or city. Frequently the psychological group grows at odds with the parent police department in a large city. Some bureaucracies create an atmosphere that fosters development of primary groups opposing the bureaucracy.

Conversely, the officer employed by a small town or rural police department has his need to feel worthwhile met by the police department, and as a result the officer remains loyal to the police department and the community. The magnitude of the difference between these two examples only becomes obvious after studying the relationships and interactions between the police departments and the respective communities.

Small town and rural officers are more likely to belong to a psychological group identifying with the police department. These officers feel and respond to their bonds to the police department and the community. The psychological group and the task group remain one and the same for the small town or rural police officer. The officer in the larger city works for a distant bureaucracy. He might feel loyalty to a small group, but only the small town or rural officer knows feelings of loyalty to and receives such personal satisfaction from belonging to a police department.

Group dynamics is another important concept which affects officers on small town and rural police departments with a greater relative frequency than it does officers in larger police departments. Group dynamics appears as the chemical phenomenon of synergism applied to a social setting. Synergism occurs when the whole seems greater than the sum of its parts. Group dynamics occur when a group of people can accomplish more acting as a group than they can as individuals.

Recall the football team example. Suppose a coach took Alabama's quarterback, OSU's center, a left tackle from the University of Texas, and so forth to build a team. Now imagine them all meeting to play against Penn State at Penn State's home stadium. The visiting team would not stand a chance because they are not a psychological group, and they cannot experience group dynamics. They remain eleven individuals performing as a physical group. They do not even form a team.

The term "team spirit" denotes psychological grouping, and the term "team effort" denotes group dynamics. Since our football team meets none of the requirements, they display neither psychological group formation nor group dynamics. Group dynamics appears as that seemingly unexplained force that emerges from within a small group of people and enables them as a group to accomplish what would otherwise seem impossible. It helps to explain why long-shot ball teams surpass their own preset high goals, win honors and titles, and break records.

One little-recognized aspect of group dynamics remains the fact that the individual infected with team effort can produce more or perform better as an individual than that same person could perform in the absence of group dynamics. Bannister, the first person to run a mile in less than four minutes, achieved the impossible only with the aid of group dynamics. Four other well-trained and superbly disciplined runners each ran a quarter mile in a planned manner and precise time to pace Bannister. Group dynamics permitted him to do something seemingly by himself which he could not accomplish without support. The team effort, not the individual, broke the impossible four-minute mile. Small town and rural police membership works in much the same way. Individual officers representing the entire police department seem able to accomplish the most difficult police tasks.

Group dynamics includes two aspects. First, the whole appears greater than the sum of its parts. The small town or rural police department can do far more as a dynamic team than a physical group the same size might accomplish. Second, the individual belonging to a dynamic group can achieve more as an individual because of his group dynamics than an individual without group dynamics might achieve. Group dynamics affect both the group's work and the individual's work. Raw numbers limit the size of psychological groups and the size of groups capable of experiencing group dynamics. The upper limits are the same, usually fifteen. The lower limits are also the same, two. By definition, a group requires at least two people. Two remain the minimum required for psychological group formation and for group dynamics. For a group to excite group dynamics, each member must enjoy easy face-to-face access to every other member. This almost never occurs in groups with more than fifteen members. A greater proportion of small town and rural police departments than big city police departments experience group dynamics infecting each and every officer. Most small town and rural police departments but very few big city police departments benefit from group dynamics.

A comical but typical bureaucratic characteristic emerges at this point. It appears as the opposite, not just the absence, of group dynamics. Fifteen remains the maximum limit in terms of group dynamics. After fifteen, strange things begin to happen: the bureaucracy counterproductive syndrome warps the desired effect. After the size of a police department passes fifteen an increasingly large and disproportionate number of officers must leave the streets to administer affairs and push paper. Conversely, this means a smaller percentage of the police department's officers will actually police. For example, Wincity claims 10,000 citizens and ten police officers. The chief likes people and enjoys policing, spending most of his time in the field. Loserville's 10,000 residents maintain a police department of eighteen. As every seasoned officer knows, perceptions can deceive. Their chief believes strongly in precise, written accountability and paper policing. He strives constantly to increase efficiency. To maintain his strict standards requires eight officers, other than the chief, so that nine, or fifty percent of the police department, work the street. Wincity fields almost ten officers while Loserville, with an 80 percent greater police department, actually puts fewer officers on he street. As the Organization and Administration chapter discusses, this is much more common than the public realizes. The rule of thumb in large cities declares that 40 to 50 percent of a police department works in administration. I found a sheriff's office with over sixty officers on the payroll, hundreds of square miles of rural area dotted with communities to police, and four officers assigned to the patrol division — not exactly a flawless example of group dynamics. The National Advisory Commission does not mention this patrol-payroll ratio anywhere in the 668 pages of its monumental *Report on Police*. The whole of a large police department is less than the sum of its parts.

In terms of group dynamics the small town or rural police department with one officer emerges as an exception. Sociologists define a group as two or more and thus claim no interest in the one officer police department. Social synergism requires at least two people for group dynamics to work its magic. This book explains the one officer police department as an important social institution, but it remains that regardless of how dynamic or truly superb this person performs as an officer, the police department and community cannot reap the benefits of group dynamics. It takes at least two people to dance, fight, make love, or generate group dynamics. While police officers might witness exceptions to the first three, no exceptions exist to the requirement of two or more for group dynamics.

Every police department, regardless of size, remains a physical group since the members dress alike, work the same area, and answer to the same employer. Social interaction occurs within virtually every police department with more than one officer. Because of the limited number of persons involved, the absence of a bureaucracy, and other reasons, social interaction occurs more often, more directly, more informally, and more personally in small town and rural police departments than it does in larger police departments. Psychological groups seem more likely to form in small town and rural police departments because those officers enjoy more face-to-face personal, intimate interaction with every other officer on the police department. This results in shared needs being fulfilled, creating a unique bonding between the officer and the police department. Sometimes the small town or rural officer and police department behave as one and the same. "Do you work for the police department?" "No Ma'am, I *am* the police department."

Group dynamics infect and affect a greater percentage of small town and rural police departments than it does other police departments. Such is possible only because the limited number of individuals involved experience direct one-to-one informal interaction; share common interests, objectives, and goals; see themselves as a group or team; and obtain satisfaction because of group membership. Group dynamics serve to provide additional energy and initiative to both the small town or rural police department and its officers.

Other explanations exist to support the group division between fifteen and sixteen. Dividing the 168-hour police week (7 × 24 = 168) by a 40-hour work week shows that 4.2 or five officers seem necessary to cover a 24-hour operation seven days a week. This five figure does not make allowances for vacations, sick time, back-up officers, or overtime. When these everyday personnel demands of shift work are considered, fourteen officers seem needed to field two officers on the street at all times.

This appears to free the fifteenth officer, the chief, for administration and management duties. Oddly enough, this frequently does not happen. It looks good on the duty roster, but in reality the chief of a small town or rural police department invariably finds himself working the streets. The working chief covers felony or high priority calls when other units cannot or his presence might help. On police departments with sixteen or more officers, the chief seldom works patrol; and on police departments with more than twenty officers, the desk chief never works the street. To produce effective policing, the chief of any police department must exhibit all the traits of a good leader. To survive, the chief of a small town or rural police department must be a good leader and a street-wise police officer.

The three major methods used to define the size of police departments involve examining, first, the number of officers employed by each police department; second, the population of jurisdictions, either the number of people in a jurisdiction or the social nature of those people; and, third, the degree of social interaction involved in police departments and between officers and community members. Using the exact number of officers employed by a police department seems the quantitative method least subject to attack, but it can mislead concerning the number of officers actually policing. Too frequently this method digresses into inappropriate, unreliable, and invalid grouping. Qualitative variables of policing comprise the major important differences between police departments of various sizes.

Synthesizing the work of sociologists, psychologists, organizational authorities, and criminal justice academicians and field practitioners defines small town and rural police departments as those local public police departments and sheriffs' offices employing fifteen or fewer full-time police officers. Some of these small town or rural police departments might also be accurately described as metropolitan, urban, surburban, exurban, rural, or nonmetropolitan. For purposes of introducing a standard into the language and to begin to name different size police departments, this book defines a small town or rural police department as one employing fewer than sixteen full-time police officers. Numerous reasons exist for this demarcation, supporting it as natural, real, logical, and not the least bit arbitrary.

All police departments with fewer than sixteen officers possess enough common variables and differ enough from all other police departments to merit grouping them together as small town and rural police departments.

Part II

DIFFERENCES BETWEEN OFFICERS
BY DEPARTMENT SIZE

Chapter 3

EDUCATION

ASSUMED differences between small town or rural police and their big city or urban counterparts are carved in stone. The mass media and popular literature have helped erect a public perception and overall image of small town and rural policing which is negative and derogatory. Objective, scholarly research and empirical measurement of these alleged differences produce many surprising results.

In some areas differences simply do not exist. Long-held beliefs and perceptions do not conform to reality. Unquestioned assumptions involve misconceptions. In these areas the small town and rural police officer and his policing remain indistinguishable from the officer or his performance in the largest of cities. Old myths must be eliminated and replaced with facts which reflect reality. The public must be educated and reprogrammed in light of this new found evidence, if an accurate picture of policing in the United States is to be presented. The more we understand and know about our police, the more effective policing we will experience and enjoy.

In other areas of the police world differences related to the size of the agencies do exist. Sometimes these differences are about what was expected, but other times these differences are completely opposite to expectations. In still other comparisons of police departments by size, it has been found that the differences or relationships are of a completely different nature or degree than was anticipated. Again, misconceptions must be corrected by public education before the full potential of policing in this country will be realized. If the public adopts a more accurate image of their local police, citizens will be less likely to harbor unreasonable expectations of the police.

It is nothing less than exciting to discover the actual differences between small town and rural police and their fraternity brothers on larger police departments. It is these very differences that will allow the isolation of certain variables. Once this is done, researchers can experiment, observe, predict, and improve future policing. Variables that fluctuate significantly with department size must be studied and subjected to the most rigorous analysis. This book does not suggest that one police department is better than another because of size. It does suggest that to improve policing, research must determine which size police departments are most likely to produce which results. That knowledge can then be used to modify policing where and when appropriate or desirable. No group of certain size police departments has a monopoly on the best way to police. The only monopoly certain size police departments have possessed in the past has been a steadfast refusal to study and learn from police departments of an extremely different size.

To state that one size police department differs from another size police department can be interpreted as the former being the deviant and the latter the norm. The reader is cautioned to guard against this bias by bearing in mind what is desireable. In some comparisons neither small nor larger police departments possess the appropriate or desired values of a variable.

The data base for this study was collected by surveying police departments in Arizona and Mississippi. On site visitations were used to interview administrators and police officers and to review records. After collection, the data were analyzed in terms of relationships among variables. The first variable to be addressed here is education.

The Wickersham Commission in 1931 was the first body to conduct a major study of police in the United States. Two of the fourteen volumes produced by the commission concerned the police. They concluded that police sorely needed more education.

August Vollmer wrote parts of the Wickersham report, and it reflected his philosophy, especially emphasizing the necessity for upgrading the police via education. Vollmer never relented in his insistence that police officers should be relatively as well educated as doctors and lawyers. He reasoned that advanced education and extensive preparation were prerequisites for entry into any professional field. Absolutely nothing has occured in the police world during the past fifty years that might indicate Vollmer's reasoning was flawed. Considerable evidence suggests the need is now greater than ever before.

In the late sixties, public opinion polls showed fear of crime was the top concern of citizens for the first time since such polling began. Twenty years later, public opinion polls indicated that crime, violence, drugs, or some combination of the three continued to be a major concern in the United States. The Law Enforcement Assistance Administration (LEAA) was established in the late sixties as part of the government's response to the nation's fear of crime. Numerous blue ribbon panels, committees, and task forces were also established to study the problems, seek solutions, and make recommendations.

One of the those committees, The National Advisory Commission on Criminal Justice Standards and Goals, produced the largest and most comprehensive study of the police ever undertaken. It bears the same title as the Wickersham report of forty years earlier, *Report on Police*. The 24 chapters of this latest *Report on Police* contain dozens of standards and recommendations. One entire chapter is devoted to education. The introduction to the education chapter once again echoes the necessity of emphasizing police education, pointing out that police officers with college experience perform better than officers with little or no college experience. This remains an ageless principle applied to the police occupation. An educated citizen is a better citizen. The more education possessed by people in a group, occupation, or country, then the stronger and healthier that group will be.

Report on Police proposed a timetable for educational standards for police officer applicants. It called for "every police agency" to require by 1982 a four-year higher education degree for initial employment. Obviously, the police have fallen way short of that goal. If the quality of policing is to be improved, then education standards must be met. Putting college educated officers into policing today will insure that the police administrators of tomorrow will be qualified. This in turn will attract more college educated people to policing.

The Law Enforcement Education Program (LEEP) was established during the same time as LEAA, offering financial assistance to police officers attending college. LEEP probably did more than any other single factor to improve police educational levels. Money often proves to be an effective incentive. LEEP was the opportunity and encouragement many officers needed. Being a sliding scale, forgiveable loan, the financial aid provided the needed encouragement for officers to stay in policing.

The major weakness of the many noble and worthwhile standards of the *Report on Police* was that they were only nonmandatory recommendations and did not have the force and power of law. Recommendations are not requirements. The medical field did not improve and earn the prestige of a profession, until they *mandated* and enforced by law certain minimum educational standards and requirements in the early part of this century. Likewise, attorneys professionalized their occupation with minimum but *mandatory* education requirements and examinations during the forties. The police field will never be able to avoid the professional requirement of enforcing minimum educational standards within their own ranks, if policing is to be considered a profession. Taking such action can be delayed for many years, as it has been for the past fifty, but the hallmarks of a professional field remain unchanged and cannot be circumvented on the road to professionalizing the police. Delay in mandating police education is Russian roulette.

L. P. Donovan's *The Municipal Police: A Rural and Urban Comparison* is the pioneer study comparing police education levels by size of department. He studied 284 small town and rural police departments and 255 urban and suburban police departments in Missouri. He used only percentages in examination of the data and no sophisticated statistical techniques. The word *significant* is not to be found in his study, but he concluded that to a limited degree urban police tended to be better educated than rural police.

His Missouri survey was completed in 1971, my Arizona survey was finished in 1975, and my Mississippi research was accomplished in 1982. The purpose of my research was then and continues to be to determine what differences exist between different size police departments and the nature of those differences.

All 32 of the small town and rural police departments in Arizona at that time were included in the 1975 study. All police departments and sheriffs' offices, large and small, were included in the 1982 Mississippi study. Data were collected by on site visits and analyzed using multiple linear regression, an advanced statistical analysis technique.

In terms of education, the findings were consistent with the literature. A statistically significant positive relationship exists between agency size and the average educational levels of police officers (see Appendix E). The larger the police department, the more education its officers will tend to claim. The average number of years of formal education earned by officers increases as the focus changes from small town and rural police departments to larger police departments. This is explained by several variables.

Larger police departments pay higher salaries and are, therefore, more attractive to recent college graduates. Most large cities have a college or university convenient to police officers, whereas many small towns and rural areas do not offer higher education opportunities with such convenience. The pressures and forces persuading police officers to obtain more education are probably felt more strongly on the larger police departments. Competition is likely a strong incentive. Officers in big cities make more money and seem more likely to feel they can afford to pay tuition.

Salary certainly plays a role in an officer's decision to pursue higher education, especially since LEEP no longer exists. Larger cities are more likely to offer education incentives in the form of financial assistance to police officers. Big-city officers tend to live where they work, while small-city officers tend to work where they live. Consequently, career-minded officers gravitate to the higher salaries where they are among strangers, while small town and rural officers work in a social environment where they are everything but strangers.

But small town and rural police officers are attending college and university classes in increasing numbers. A criminal justice student of mine commutes ninety miles one way to classes. A former airline stewardess, she is now a police chief of a nine officer police department and a member of Alpha Phi Sigma, the national criminal justice honor society.

Both the Arizona and Mississippi studies found that educational levels of small town and rural police are increasing faster than educational levels of the general population. Evidence also suggests that the gap between educational levels of small town police and big city police is decreasing.

Comparing results of the three studies, the overall average number of years of police education ranked between twelve and thirteen years in each state. These averages are only slightly above state-mandated minimum requirements. Education levels rise perhaps only to meet the absolute minimums and then hover there. This strengthens the argument for requiring a four-year college degree of all police officers. The position that a police officer does not need a college degree appears no longer defensible.

Earlier, the mandated education standards for doctors and lawyers were mentioned. However, about 25,000 medical doctors practice in the United States today with bogus credentials, and some states still license attorneys who have no college training. Using the same logic, a college degree is not absolutely essential to practice law or medicine. However, if it is desirable to employ police officers who can communicate clearly and effectively, who can comprehend the everchanging social structure of an increasingly complex culture, who can reason with analytical ability, and who possess genuine intellectual curiosity and humanistic values, then a four-year college degree must be the minimum acceptable standard.

A few decades ago the required education for most police officers was above the average of those policed. Then the general public's educational level rose to equal that of the police. Now, educational levels of police are generally below those of the people they serve. No other single factor explains so much police ineffectiveness and frustration. There remains no doubt as to the causal relationship here. The general population's dissatisfaction with the police increases in direct proportion to the distance that the education of the people exceeds that of the police. People quickly shun incompetent physicians, lawyers, auto mechanics, and all others who give the image of being ill-prepared to perform their roles. No reason exists to view police and policing differently.

To say that the failure of traditional police methods in big cities cannot be explained is to ignore the differences in educational levels between the police and the policed. Higher education of police is the only key to effective policing, crime reduction, and crime prevention. One prediction holds that by the year 2000, police education in the computer science field alone will lag so far behind criminals that the police will be totally ineffective as investigators. Some of the more cynical officers working today will say that situation already exists in some areas. The prognosticators are only ten years behind the officer on the beat.

While it is true that police educational levels are increasing, the relative rate must be considered for a proper perspective. It is also a fact that educational levels of the general population are increasing at a faster rate. The public is outstripping the police in education. The slow or dull cannot police the quick or sharp. Education is the only key to effective policing, and the only way to make the key work is with legislated, college-level minimums.

August Vollmer and the 1973 *Report on Police* were correct in associating police education with police performance. Police educational levels must be raised significantly, if improved police performance and crime reduction are to become reality.

The common image of small town and rural police officers places the education of the sheriff's deputy below that of the small town municipal police officer and slightly above that of a hard boiled egg. The literature did not distinguish by type of agency, whether police department or sheriff's office, when addressing educational levels.

Empirical research shows there is no relationship between educational achievement and type of agency. Police officers employed by a sheriff's office will not vary significantly, in terms of education, from officers employed by municipal police departments. The false stereotypes about differences between small town and big city police have too often carried over to presumed differences between municipal and county police. It is reassuring to learn that county police have as much education as that of municipal police.

This negative stereotype is a transfer of beliefs. The unfounded but common prejudice that rural people are lazy and dumb misfits is carried over to distort one's view of rural police. Sheriffs' officers frequently police rural areas and therefore suffer as victims of prejudicial thoughts and discriminatory behavior.

Television programs have pictured the rural deputy, or police officer, as the typical country clown for decades. Empirical evidence now indicates that such stereotyping is completely without foundation. The educational levels of police officers do not differ between municipal and county officers. If we want to view our police realistically, then we must refrain from all actions or statements that perpetuate the many unfounded myths about small town and rural police.

The key to improving policing is education. The price of the key is a lack of mandated standards. To gain health one must give up illness and everything that accompanies it. To gain improved policing, the luxury of no mandated minimum educational standards must be surrendered. The luxury of illness is too expensive.

The American Medical Association, the American Bar Association, and national teachers' groups improved their respective occupations with uniform, mandated minimum educational requirements. The middle 1980s witnessed a growing concern and lobby for a nationwide licensing of big truck operators. Nursing experienced an educational explosion in the sixties parallel to the one in policing, but nursing followed through with enforced standards, policing did not.

The days are over, forever, of an individual reading one or two books on the subject, studying briefly, and becoming a doctor, lawyer, nurse, or school teacher. In the mideighties Texas required 1,500 hours of training for cosmetologists but only 320 training hours for police officers. Sadly, some police officers today have never read a book in their entire life. Prior to the sixties, only a select few could become police officers. Today, regardless of what is told police academy graduating classes, virtually anyone can become a police officer.

Unlike other occupational fields, policing is stuck in the quagmire of a refusal to legislate and enforce education standards. Other occupational fields managed to plan, organize, persist, follow through, and emerge downstream with a framework to upgrade their vocation. Defying all laws of evolution, policing has slipped into neutral, or worse, park. To avoid what future historians will surely call the dark ages of policing, the vocation must take immediate action towards adopting nationwide uniform standards. The first standard must be education.

Virtually anyone can be trained to cuff and stuff a doper. But to do it legally; write a clear, concise, accurate, and complete report; and testify in an articulate, convincing, ethical manner require skills and logic acquired chiefly by experiencing higher education. Conviction rates remain much higher for police officers with college degrees. High arrest rates without subsequent high conviction rates are worse than worthless. Arrests without convictions waste money and human resources, clog the justice process, jeopardize due process rights, and further erode the public's confidence in their police and justice system. The public deserves predictable, standard practices within each public service occupation. The police are no exception. Citizens deserve and need police officers with more higher education.

Computers, technology, law, and many other facets of our society continue to change and improve our daily lives and lifestyles. Computers have accelerated many occupations in their evolutionary development. Police tend to be very conservative and status quo oriented for many reasons. They resist change. Most police departments do not have a computer; and, of those that do, most use them for record retrieval only.

The times they are a changin'; and police must change, too. It is impossible to change the police without that magic key. The most expensive newly installed computer at the local police department is only as valuable as the educational preparation of those police officers using it. Computer programmers without police experience might perform miracles in other fields, but they will fail in full utilization of the police computer. This person must be bilingual, able to speak both computer and police.

Officers who have earned a baccalaureate receive fewer personnel complaints, more commendations, more promotions, and earn more over a career. They also police better. They are the next generation of police. As more college graduates progress up through the ranks into the highest levels of police administration, their leadership and the college-educated officers they insist on hiring, will result in a greatly improved quality of policing. Retreads, those veteran police officers who return to school and earn a college degree, are in a middle generation. Too frequently they succumb to the temptation to go with the flow and not make waves. Tradition is the most dreadful enemy of police innovation and progress. I once worked for a police department where officers would sarcastically recite, "Seventy years of tradition, unmarred by progress."

Policing has never been improved from within. Retreads do some good and increase efficiency in a few cases. However, each time in the past that police evolution improved, it was because of a new breed of recruit entering and infecting the occupation. Policing on a nationwide scale can be improved only from outside forces. Improvements in policing across the United States will be significant, profound, and visible as more and more college educated men and women enter the occupation, as more college graduates rise to executive positions and exert more influence, and as more mandates require college education for entry into the field.

Chapter 4

RACE, SEX, TRAINING, AGE, PHYSICAL FITNESS, SALARY, CAREER ORIENTATION

THE POLICE have always been a very close-knit, clannish fraternity. They are charged with maintaining the status quo and not with making drastic, sudden changes in society. Additionally, police have almost always recruited from the working class. For these and other reasons, police tend to be traditional and conservative in their political persuasion. They resist change and are very suspicious of new policies or programs that break with established customs. White flight from the big cities to the suburbs and rural areas along with the more deeply-rooted values and strongly cherished mores of small towns and rural areas have served to further reinforce and strengthen the traditional beliefs and conservative practices of the nonmetropolitan United States. Yet again, the police mirrored their parent community.

Race and sex have always been four-letter words when recruiting police applicants. After the civil rights movement of the sixties, police departments were very slow to recruit nonwhite personnel as would be expected given their conservative nature. Small town and rural police departments were the slowest of the slow, frequently refusing to hire nonwhites. Change came slowly and painfully. Affirmative action legislation and law suits involving racial discrimination in employment helped to desegregate the larger police departments; but many small town and rural police departments continued into the eighties with only white, male officers. Gradually, this is being corrected as more recruits with college or university degrees work their way into the ranks and administration of small town and rural police departments. In defense of tradition, it has been observed that some of these small towns and rural communities contain no racial minorities; and, therefore, an all white police department is not necessarily a sign of racial discrimination. The small town police department should be an accurate sample of the racial composition of that town.

Recruiting and hiring females as police officers has proven to be more controversial for many small town and rural police departments than employment of racial minorities. Since policing was one of the very last occupations to hire nonwhites and small town and rural police have been the last subgroup within the occupation to change, apparently the same reluctance will prevail concerning the issue of women in policing. The question of whether or not women could perform police tasks as well as men was spotlighted during the women's movement of the seventies. Experience with women officers has caused us to realize that that is not the real issue. The real issue is in what areas of policing will women outperform men and how might the skills and abilities of women be best utilized in the police environment.

The one and only indisputable difference between the sexes in police work is upper-body strength. On the average, men possess greater upper-body strength than do women. Diehards use this fact tirelessly when explaining why women should not be police officers. The difficulty with this argument is that upper-body strength, like height, has never been demonstrated to be a prerequisite or requirement for police work. Since upper-body strength is not a job-related requirement in police work, the individual personal opinion of the police chief is the only explanation for so few police departments employing female officers. Until upper-body strength is demonstrably linked to police performance, the courts will continue to rule in favor of equal employment opportunities for women in policing.

Upper-body strength has been shown to be directly related to job performance in fire fighting. A fire fighter must be able to drag a heavy hose up a ladder and carry a person down a ladder. Screening tests for fire fighters have been pretty much standardized. Only those women with the necessary upper-body strength are accepted. Both men and women lacking such minimum abilities are rejected as potential fire fighters.

A police department employing about 100 officers serves a city with a population that is about 40 percent nonwhite near my hometown. That police department, in January of 1987, had no nonwhite officers on the payroll and only two females. In contrast, another nearby small town with 80 percent white population and a police department with fewer than sixteen officers has employed at least one nonwhite officer for years but steadfastly refuses to hire women. Those who argue that women have no place in policing or that women cannot police as well as men are oftentimes the very same ones who argue that a woman's place is in the home and not in the work place.

A small town, East Texas police chief once told me that if he had his "druthers," which he quickly pointed out he did not have, he would hire nothing but women. They are much more conscientious and concerned with performance since they know they are being watched, according to him. He also believed that women can be just as suspicious as men and that they do not exhibit overconfidence as often as men. His attitude about hiring women as police officers was a very rare exception, but time might prove him to be insightful about the differences of the genders in police performance.

Superior upper-body strength of men might also lead to overconfidence and too many fights. Often women officers have made statements about having to use brains instead of muscles. When I was a boy, a sheriff's deputy in my home county had only one arm. Yet, he worked the streets alone; and his colleagues all acknowledged that he was a superb officer. He was forced to use his intellect and never grew lax with the knowledge that as a last resort he could always enjoy fighting his way out of any situation. He was as brazen as any other officer. I've seen him roust drunks with most effective results. It is definitely possible that as more women enter policing, certain traditional tactics and methods will be replaced with more intelligent and humane, and less physical and forceful, procedures.

In the literature on nonverbal communication, it has been suggested that women are better at reading and interpreting body language than are men. Evidence shows that women are more sensitive to sound, scents, and touching. This is thought to be a genetic trait which permits mothers to understand the needs of an infant. Many fathers have been amazed at the seemingly magic way their wives know the cause of their baby's crying.

This has profound implications for policing. The effective officer must be ever vigilant and use all powers of observation. Imagine the possibility of time and experience yielding evidence which further suggests that women officers are more vigilant. All this also lends credibility to the term: a woman's intuition.

Intuition has been used for decades in police work. It is a combination of education, training, and experience as applied to the totality of circumstances surrounding a particular police situation. Now, if a woman's gender improves her intuition, she would have a distinct advantage over a man in certain police tasks. Good examples of this would be those situations where early detection of potential escalating hostilities would assist in defusing the explosiveness and preventing violence. Perhaps a woman's ability to better read and understand body language is a compensation for a lack of upper body strength. Just perhaps, the female officer would not need the upper body strength as often. Maybe women are better than men at preventative policing.

The mere suggestion that women might outperform men in some police tasks is at once both frightening and intimidating to many in the macho, swaggering, man's world of policing. But regardless of fears and apprehensions, the possibility does exist and must be researched and examined carefully if a greater potential for policing is to be realized.

The calming effect that the presence of a member of the opposite sex has on an individual has been observed for many years. Public school teachers generally prefer a class balanced with both boys and girls, over a class of all one gender. This phenomenon was mentioned when the Voyager, the first aircraft to fly nonstop around the globe unrefueled, landed on Christmas Eve, 1986, with its one man and one woman crew. They were aviation pioneers pushing the limits in extremely cramped quarters. For nine days they worked, fought the unknown and unexpected, flew, and experienced all emotions in what was described as a horizontal telephone booth. It was suggested that having two pilots of different sexes contributed significantly to the success of that historic endeavor. The Russians have included women in their space flights longer than we have.

Sociologists, psychologists, and others naturally explain this phenomenon in terms of their respective disciplines. Even biologists contribute. Body smells, or pheromones, have long been known to exist in animals and play a definite role in their behavior. The most recent research now indicates that some human behavior may be unconsciously influenced by the scents of others. As humorous as it might be, this topic, too, like so many others in police science, needs more investigation and study. We need to sniff it out. I would be the first to confess that I believe women smell better than men, but the implication for future policing is much more serious.

Since males are responsible for the vast majority of violent crime in this country, the promising but unexplored potential of women police officers must be examined in all its minutiae. If women police can detect and identify impending violence and contribute more to reducing it by their mere presence, then preventive action can be taken and lives can be saved. If women police can better detect and identify potential violence, then greater emphasis must be placed on the recruitment and retention of female officers.

A possible calming effect of the female voice is thought by some to have a definite place in police work. Again, the most frequently cited illustration is the situation involving a hostile male or rapidly escalating dispute. It is believed by some that a female officer's voice has a tranquilizing effect. Her presence and uniform commands attention to authority while her feminine voice placates and soothes. Likewise, some feel that the mere presence of a woman officer will avert a physical combative situation, possibly because of the learned reluctance of many men to fight a woman.

The social chemistry of a police department must be representative of the people it serves, if it is to be effective. More women must be recruited into policing careers and a more equitable gender ratio established, regardless of the debate about their precise abilities or roles. Virtually all cities, small or large, are about equally proportioned by sex. Their police departments should reflect a similar ratio. The only defensible exceptions would be those remote rural or small town police departments where the concensus of the total populace is that women have no place in police work. In these areas women police are rejected by the public, male and female alike, and cannot survive.

Predictably, few women seek employment with such agencies and so few are successful that they remain statistically insignificant. Few women seek such employment in those areas, just as few nonwhites seek employment in all white communities. But these are all exceptions. The rule is embarrassing to the occupation. More women must be hired in all sizes of police departments. Police administrators must take the initiative, actively recruit, and hire more women. This will prevent policing from being among the last occupations to lower sexist barriers, make the police more like their communities, and thereby greatly enhance the quality of policing.

Of all the myths perpetuated by the media about police and policing, none is more prevalent than the image of the small town or rural officer who obviously has never received any training. This myth forms the very core of the overall derogatory labeling endured by small town and rural police. Nearly all the undesirable attributes of this pitiful, stereotypical officer can be traced back to a lack of training. Such false perceptions are reinforced with the opposite picture of the big city officer as super-dynamic — a quick solution for every problem. The implication is unavoidable: the big city officer seems superbly trained. A television series was based on the exploits of police officers in the Los Angeles Police Academy, fearless champions of justice. During the same night the TV viewer could select between two other police shows, both depicting the clumsy, stupid misadventures of small town or rural police officers. Fortunately, for policing in general, and small town and rural police departments in particular, empirical evidence now exists which refutes these popular misconceptions.

"Pre-employment training for police should be comparable in quality to that provided for lawyers, doctors, and other professionals" (Kobetz, 1980, p. 1). Such lofty ideals sound as if they came from contemporary times, or at least as recent as the *Report on Police* in 1973. August Vollmer expressed such visionary requirements more than half a century ago. Today, it remains for the most part just that, a vision.

In the early thirties the first major study of our police was undertaken by the Wickersham Commission. It exposed the huge police training deficit. It was the first of many calls for more and better police training. In the late sixties and early seventies the alarms were repeated and the cries for improved quantity and quality of police training were echoed.

The monumental 1973 *Report on Police* suggested standards, minimums, types, and other guidelines in a clear, straightforward format. The chapter on training in the *Report on Police* is by far the longest of twelve chapters dealing with effective police service. It recommends that every police officer should have a minimum of 400 hours of basic police training initially and a minimum of forty hours of inservice training each year therafter.

Many years later these well researched recommendations remain largely ignored. Although most states did have some mandated training in 1980, those with required training averaged less than a 300-hour requirement. As recently as 1980 a few states remained with no legislated minimum police training requirement.

The variable of police training is not unlike those of police education and salaries. We expect a lot from our police, but we really want something for nothing, or at least a twofold return on our dollar. The police are expected to protect life and property, reduce crime, enforce the law, serve the public, identify, locate, and arrest criminals and law violators, and perform a myriad of other duties, all with relatively few hours of training. In Texas, as of this writing, my barber must have almost five times more training to cut my hair than is required of a police officer to carry a firearm and throw me in jail. This is not to belittle barbers' training but rather to draw attention to the ridiculous inadequacy of police training.

It is becoming increasingly more difficult to distinguish between police training and police education. In fact there should be a lot of overlap. Training has been defined as the introduction to an occupation and the development of related skills. Education includes the attitudes, philosophies, rationales, and logic associated with a field of study. Police must have a considerable degree of both if they are to deal with and communicate effectively with people and people's problems. Training tells the new officer the needed elements of a legal arrest and how to best accomplish a safe and uneventful arrest. Education can provide the logic and history of that particular law and the intent behind the framing of a particular law.

The old distinctions between training and education are disappearing along with generalizations about white, blue, and pink collar classifications. Advanced technology, social conditions, and the information explosion contribute to a merging of education and training.

But when does the officer learn when to arrest? Frequently the officer receives absolutely no introduction to the complex but vital concept of discretion, until he is forced to deal with it on the street. Some academies at larger departments prohibit instructors from discussing discretion. One large police department academy session I attended included drill in chanting, "Attitude does not matter." There is little wonder the seasoned field training officer (FTO) tells the fresh academy graduate to forget everything he's learned in the police academy. Attitude does matter; and the recruit knows it, regardless of what he is made to repeat.

Imagine the results of medical training without any discussion of discretion. There would be untold thousands of totally unnecessary and damaging operations. Medical students study the use of placebos and later as doctors skillfully employ that knowledge to relieve pain and suffering and provide contentment. Many police officers painfully learn at great expense the vital concept of desirable deception. With no concern as to whether it is training or education, medical doctors are taught they must sometimes deceive people. No police officer has ever been formally taught constructive deception but instead is frequently reminded to be "honest in both thought and deed." The reality of street policing on any size police department dictates otherwise. He lies not only to frightened children and worried parents, accident victims and dying people, theft victims and neighborhood residents, but street people, suspects, criminals and straight arrow citizens, like you and me, as well.

The doctor deceives when it will help the patient. The police officer deceives when it best serves justice, or, like the doctor, to relieve pain and suffering and provide contentment.

Doctors and firefighters alike for many years have studied prevention techniques. The best way to treat a medical problem or fight a fire is to prevent it. Larger police departments have crime prevention programs and police community relations (PCR) bureaus. They are relatively ineffective since they fail to realize that the patrol officer on the street is the best and ultimately only real PCR and crime prevention officer. Yet almost without exception, the recruit receives inadequate or no training in this crucial area. Like doctors and firefighters, police should attempt to put themselves out of business via prevention — crime prevention.

Policing is, in its most oversimplified form, nothing more than interpersonal communication. The officer on any police department must be an effective communicator to be an effective police officer. There is a strong positive correlation between an officer's interpersonal communication effectiveness and his policing effectiveness. Dr. Randolph Hicks, one of the foremost authorities on the subject, concluded in an empirical study in the 1980s that more training in interpersonal communication was sorely needed. This was not as surprising as his finding that police in general perceive a need for this kind of training. The police know their weaknesses but for a variety of reasons are unable to correct them.

Police training is woefully lacking in vital areas such as discretion, crime prevention, and interpersonal communication. What, and how, then, are police officers taught? Almost all initial training can be identified with six general categories: patrol and investigation, law, the criminal justice system, human values and problems, administration, and police proficiency. The major criticism that can be made is simply that there is too little, in all six areas, in police departments of every size.

Training is commonly categorized by its location in an officer's career. Recruit training most often consists of the state mandated minimum number of weeks of basic police subjects drawn from the six general areas, with concentration on the law and the more dangerous and glamorous. Recruit training does not vary by size of police department. Once out of the academy, the officer is paired with an experienced field training officer (FTO) for a few weeks or months. FTO programs possess enormous potential. They can, and frequently do, make or break an officer. They serve as a bridge between the classroom and the street. A good FTO program can cement a strong bond between theory and application. A bad FTO program can cause new officers with potential to leave the occupation entirely, or remain as worthless employees.

Police departments with fewer than sixteen officers have difficulty supporting a lengthy FTO period. Police departments with fewer than nine or ten officers frequently have no FTO program. The best FTO programs are invariably found in police departments with more than fifteen officers.

In-service training is the third type. It varies from a few hours to a month or even more but usually is less than a week in duration. In all three types, in police departments of all sizes, the quantity of training is often not sufficient. The quality of training in all three types is not always acceptable. The quantity and quality of police training vary too much.

There is too little time spent on many very important subjects and too many subjects totally ignored. There is too little time spent, on the average, in initial recruit training and too little time spent on refresher training. Too many police departments are incestuous in the training and education of their officers, using instructors exclusively from within their ranks. More police departments must utilize outside resources and expertise. Using instructors from within might improve efficiency; but such practices stifle originality and initiative, encouraging mediocrity and limiting alternatives for the officer. Too little training time is devoted to inservice training, especially for the patrol officer.

Too little time and effort is invested in the training of our police. Considering the education and training they currently receive, they produce almost miraculous results. The return on the investment of increasing police training would be exponential. Policing will show significant improvement only after police training and education show significant improvement.

A look at other countries shows that police training in the United States does not compare well. All police recruits in Japan in 1974 received 52 weeks of training, while their counterparts in the United States averaged only six weeks, with some receiving no training whatsoever. Irish police recruits are trained for 18 weeks and then return for an additional four weeks training after they have worked for a year. French police recruit training is six months long. Police recruits in West Germany and Denmark are trained for three years. Although this does involve some on-the-job training, it is mostly theoretical. In England and Wales the recruit is kept in training for almost all of the first two years of service. Scottish police recruits are trained for eight weeks, work for one year, and then receive another six weeks of training.

Police executives and administrators in other countries also receive more training. The National Police College of England and Wales (Bramshill) offers high level education for future police leaders. The Scottish National Police College (Tulliallian Castle) offers command type courses from five weeks to three months in length.

The Central Police College in Taipei, Taiwan remains the world leader in police training and in educating police administrators. It has all the trademarks of a university, even a graduate program; but it caters exclusively to police. Another former Berkeley officer, Dr. V. A. Leonard, proposed a central police university for the United States. Although the magnitude of such a project seems almost unthinkable to some, the August Vollmer University might prove Dr. Leonard's suggestion best. Such a facility will serve the best interests of all police departments, regardless of size, and therein lies the soundest promise for improving policing in the United States. Such a university could meet the special needs of small town and rural police and the unique problems of larger police departments with custom tailored programs and courses in much the same manner as a modern-day university trains geologists, social workers, and chemists.

One glaring difference between foreign police systems and ours is the theme of police service as a career. Foreign police departments train recruits as though they will remain in police work for a career. Our police departments train recruits as though they might quit next month. In the vast majority of those other countries just mentioned, policing is considered to be a vocation and a career. Too often in the United States, policing is considered to be just another job. Both the public and the police view policing as just another work-a-day job, maybe more exciting, certainly more unpredictable. But in the final analysis, it is just another job; and very few officers would hesitate to jump at a higher salary or more attractive offer in another occupation.

The incorporation of standards and requirements of advanced education and training for all police officers would serve many purposes.

High mandated standards of education and training, much higher than the current average, would move the police field much closer to being recognized as a real profession. In spite of all the cries and demands for professional status, policing will not be considered a professional occupation until it polices its own training and education. High mandated standards would help turn a take-it-or-leave-it job into a worthwhile career. Bright young people would see a career with a future. Borrowing the Navy's theme, policing could be advertised for what it really can be, more than just a job — an adventure. With advanced training and education, young officers would be justifiably proud; and they would certainly be very cautious about engaging in any activity or behavior which might jeopardize their employment. Today when a young officer faces the temptation to accept a bribe, beat a prisoner, or steal, he too often realizes that the worst consequence possible is the loss of his job. Big deal — getting another job is easy. But to face losing a career — well, that's another consideration altogether.

Policing in general in the United States has required no more than a high school degree for over 25 years, while the educational level of the public served by the police continues to rise above twelve years. Mandated police education and training requirements would correct this imbalance and give the police confidence in themselves. They would then possess the knowledge, skills, confidence, and pride necessary for improved performance. One begets the other. The first observable result of tough education-training requirements for our police would be the most important: improved police performance and a safer, healthier community environment. This would be one giant step forward towards the police acquiring professional status. A rising tide lifts all boats. All police departments, from the very smallest to the largest would benefit from a police university in the United States. But the real beneficiaries would be U.S. citizens. It is an idea whose time has come.

Examining the 1982 Mississippi study indicates that the empirical findings regarding education-training were remarkable in two ways. Contrary to the literature, and therefore expectations, no difference was found between the amount of officers' training by size of police department. Secondly, it was surprising to find officers in Mississippi, a state with no minimum training requirement at that time, averaged more hours of training than did officers in the 39 states with a mandated minimum training less than five years prior.

Contrary to the literature, the 1982 study found no relationship between the number of officers employed by a police department and the training average of those officers (see Appendix C). Even the National Advisory Commission of Criminal Justice Standards and Goals wrote in *Report on Police* " . . . police training is likely to remain poor in comparison to other professions. This is especially true in smaller agencies"

(p. 380). The tone and content of this statement and the literature were wrong. Unfortunately, these misstatements served only to nourish and perpetuate myths and false stereotypes about small town and rural police.

In the pioneer 1982 study, measureable testable evidence suggested absolutely no foundation in reality for discriminating among different size police departments in terms of assumed differences in training. Officers belonging to the smallest police departments will possess as much training, on the average, as officers working with larger police departments.

Before this study the literature was based on nothing more than conjecture, assumptions, and long-held mistaken beliefs. Perhaps now the police field can begin to cleanse itself of this unfounded prejudice. Police administrators, scholars, and writers must now act in concert to convince the public that small town and rural police are not the redheaded, snaggle-toothed stepchildren they were once thought to be.

To analize the data, an intercorrelation matrix was generated. To be significant at the .05 level on a one-tailed test, with 28 degrees of freedom, the value of r had to be equal to or greater than .306. The calculated value of r was .2361. Therefore, it was concluded that there was not a significant positive relationship between the training mean of law enforcement officers and agency size.

The other unexpected finding was the relatively high number of training hours police possessed in the absence of any state requirements. This survey found several officers with no high school degree or equivalent, a few with less than six or seven years of formal education, and a few who were functionally illiterate. Yet in spite of such horrible data the overall training hours averaged higher than states with legislated minimums. Astounding! Less than 10 percent of all the officers had received no police training.

In contrast to those with no training, the average number of formal, classroom police training hours was very high. In 1978, of 39 states reporting mandated training, basic requirements varied from a low of three weeks to a high of twelve weeks, averaging seven weeks. This research found an average of 7.81 weeks in a state with no mandated police training requirement. This finding seems even more startling in light of the fact that only three police academies existed in the state at that time. There are a number of explanations as to why police officers, in a state with only three academies and no required training, would average more training than the required average of other states.

The national average of seven weeks required training may be well below what officers actually possess. Many academies have recruit programs considerably longer than the state required minimums. If that is the case, then the average of 7.81 weeks might be below, not above, national average. Much more research is certainly needed in this area to determine not just the state minimums, but how much training police today actually possess.

During the survey, I met several officers and heard of many more, who had received their training while employed by a police department in another state. Policing remains one of the few occupations where a vagabond tradesman can enjoy a change of scenery and add new friendships and memories every few years. If this is the case, then the mean hours of training officers actually have is not significantly different from mandated minimums. The great majority of the available evidence supports this position. It is believed that the average number of training hours officers possess on a state wide basis will be remarkably close to the mandated minimum. In this arrangement the minimum becomes the average, so that a ceiling effect is created.

The question then becomes whether state minimums increase training or the ceiling effect retards training. Is the wino's bottle half empty or half full? This research answered that question. A state with no minimums boasts an average greater than the national average. Rumor now has it that because of traveling distances to a central academy and the state's overall economy, the new mandated minimum will be less than six weeks. A replication study conducted ten years later should expect to find the average below 7.81 weeks. The ceiling effect will lower the average. The wino's bottle is both half empty and half full. Police training nationwide is either adequate or less than adequate. De Facto police training of street patrol officers on a nationwide scale is not adequate. The bottle is not full.

Consequently, small town and rural police will no longer fade the heat alone. They must now share the spotlight with police departments of all sizes. Small town and rural police officers have no less training than officers serving with police departments of sixteen or more officers. Our police, generally, remain undertrained and undereducated. Nationwide standards at either the state or federal level must be enacted. Current minimums must be increased many times over. Curricula must be researched, refreshed, refined, supplemented, improved, and greatly expanded. Both the quantity and quality of police training must be increased.

A former Berkeley police officer, Samuel G. Chapman, points out that those who protest federally mandated police training minimums argue that such would lead to excesses in the concentration of police power, a threat to our concepts of self government and local control. Chapman also mentions the opposing viewpoint. Nationwide minimum standards would result in uniformity of service.

These suggestions are not new. They were first germinated more than three-fourths of a century ago by the chief of a small town police department, August Vollmer. Then they echoed with the Wickersham Commission (Vollmer wrote much of the material about police for the Wickersham Commission) and resounded in the National Advisory Commission on Criminal Justice Standards and Goals. Not to be outdone, the Police Foundation poured old wine into a new bottle and labeled it *The Quality of Police Education.* But so many endorsements from such distinguished sources only strengthen the call. Old wine is the best. The need for more and better police training is more pronounced now than ever before.

These recommendations are not new. But the opportunity costs of ignoring them much longer will be catastrophic. All of these recommendations must be implemented only if we in the United States want to enjoy a safe, sane, secure and near crime-free society in which to pursue health and happiness with our constitutional freedoms. Police training and education are already a cornerstone of our national agenda. They must be recognized as such before we as a nation can realize our full potential.

By now even the reader with no police orientation or knowledge can accurately predict what the literature and media has projected regarding the relationship between the variables training and age in the police world. It has always been assumed that small town and rural police departments were heavily populated with tired and retired people who had little or no training; and all the bright, young, well-trained officers worked with the larger agencies. We lead ourselves to believe that the younger officers will be the ones with the most training. Again our assumptions are unfounded and false.

Research in the 1980s indicated no relationship exists between the variables age and training. The older officers do not have significantly more, or less, training that the younger officers have. The literature and popular perceptions do not conform to reality. No empirical evidence could be found in an exhaustive search to support a conclusion that training varied with age. Dr. Elizabeth Cross, in her landmark book, *Adults as Learners,* writes that past educational achievements are a much better predictor than age of future educational achievements. The officer who constantly volunteers for every training session or school possible is not likely to come from one certain age group.

The wise small town or rural police administrator identifies this individual who is attracted to training and utilizes him as the department training officer. This person must also have good communication and teaching skills, or at least the potential to become an effective instructor. The small town or rural police agency then immerses this officer in as much training as possible and affordable. He returns and teaches others. This multiplication of education-training permits all to learn and share from the experiences of one. In theory the entire police department attends every school and class which the departmental training officer attends. On larger police departments the homicide detective attends the speciality courses on murder, and the auto theft detective attends the classes on the latest investigation techniques in his field. This is fine as far as it goes, but only those two officers benefit from the training. Utilizing the department training officer concept, every officer on a small town or rural police department will be exposed to this new knowledge and hence be in a position to profit from it.

The 1980s research also found no difference between the hours of training an officer has and the type of agency, police department or sheriff's office, employing the officer. In some states one might be tempted, after only a cursory review, to conclude that officers working for the county have more, or less, training than officers employed by a municipal police department. Such a conclusion might be accurate for a few agencies based on limited observations. It would be a fallacy of inductive reasoning, however, to conclude that the amount of training officers possess is predictable by the type of agency to which they belong. Research done for this book also suggests such a conclusion would be an invalid generalization. Peace officers employed by a police department will average no more, or no less, training than peace officers employed by a sheriff's office.

Perhaps the most common image of the small town and rural police officer is that of the older, overweight officer. Oftentimes the younger more athletic officer is associated with the larger, more urban department. Another myth about the variations among different size police departments is about to go ten-seven for the last time.

No empirical evidence could be found indicating any correlation between the average age of officers and the size of the employing agency. This study concluded, in contrast to the very limited literature on the subject, that no statistical significant relationship exists between the ages of officers and the number of officers on a police department (see Appendix C).

Some might reason that older officers are attracted to small town and rural policing, assuming there is less real police work; and that younger officers are drawn to the larger police departments by the opportunity to engage in real police work. Policing is an action-oriented occupation, and this is a tempting explanation. In the field one might recall selected cases where older officers changed employment to move to a small town or rural police department, or a younger officer left a smaller police department for the lights, glamor, excitment, and action promised by the big city.

Small town and rural police mirror the communities they serve in terms of age. This is an integral facet of the model small town and rural police department. The police are indistinguishable from the community they police. The police represent the community in small town and rural environments. The police are a valid sample, an accurate representation of the population in these areas. So in retirement communities and small towns with few young people, it is not surprising to find the average age of police officers almost identical to the citizens' average age. I found one small city in Southern Arizona with seven officers and the chief, at 64, was the youngest man on the police department. Likewise, many small towns consist almost entirely of younger people and will reflect the same in their police departments.

A review of the literature led me to expect a negative relationship between agency size and the average age of officers. The study concluded that no such relationship exists. Officers on small town and rural police departments are not more likely to be younger or older because of the size of the police department. There is not a significant relationship between the age mean and agency size.

A significant negative relationship exists between age and education. The older the officer, the less formal schooling he will likely claim. The younger officers will probably have more formal education. Surely, a major explanation for this is the information explosion. The technology revolution paved the way for the information explosion and a greater emphasis on education. Older police have never experienced the pressure to increase their education that the younger officers have lived with. The percentage of young people attempting higher education increases with each generation.

This study found that when agency size was controlled for, a significant correlation emerged between age and type of agency. Sheriffs' officers were significantly older. Several explanations beg for attention and study. Perhaps it will be found that differences exist in the recruitment practices of sheriffs' officers and police departments. A police agency can only hire from its pool of applicants, which may result from a recruitment program or practice. More study is needed.

Since sheriffs' deputies tend to be older than municipal officers, one might speculate that sheriffs' officers would have more military experience. That is precisely what this research found. Police employed with sheriffs' offices had significantly more military experience than commissioned personnel with police departments. The most obvious explanation is the most logical. The study was conducted about eight years after the Vietnam war and the younger officers were too young to have served in the military when that was expected. Research interests concerning military experience and policing have waned in recent times with the growing number of police recruits without military experience. It has become something of a mute question. Age explains military experience. The real issue is not sheriffs' deputies having more military experience than municipal officers. The real issue and concern here is why do officers employed by sheriffs' offices tend to be older than officers employed by police departments.

No correlation was found between military experience and agency size (see Appendix C). Small town and rural police departments did not tend to have more or fewer officers with military experience. Again, age enters the picture. Military experience is a function of age, in the police world. Because age was not related to agency size it would seem to be improbable that military experience and agency size would be related.

It is not known if any relationship exists between the physical fitness of officers and agency size. It is known that police recruits are in very good physical condition and then over a period of years, their physical fitness rapidly deteriorates. Officers go from above average to below average in terms of health and physical condition. Officers on certain size police departments might meet with more encouragement and reinforcement to stay in shape. Police officers often work rotating shifts, and sleep studies have repeatedly documented the harmful effects of shiftwork on health.

Many officers aggravate this situation by staying awake all day when they finish a morning shift prior to their weekend. The officer does this to reenter the normal cycle of the rest of the world, family, and friends.

This practice is rationalized with the idea of "making it up" that night. In health terms the officer loses eight hours, or one sleep cycle, of sleep each time this is done. Sleep is essential to good health and sleeplessness, regardless of the rationale, is detrimental.

The fast food, junk food, unbalanced diet, and eating habits of police officers are both well known and well documented. The nutrition often ranges from less than adequate to endangering. Too few officers, on all police departments, have ever given serious consideration to the difference between hamburgers cooked on a flat surface and those cooked over an open flame or grill that permits the grease to escape. Too many officers give their peers reason to kid them about being knife and fork police.

Many superb books have been written about the dangers of police work, violence, shootings, car stops, family fights, and officers killed in the line of duty. Yet, many more officers die every year from heart attacks than from all violent means combined. The absence of research and study in this area is a crime by omission.

Police are trained intensely in so-called areas of real police work such as, felon apprehension, felony car stops, family disputes, and shoot-don't shoot situations; and well they should be. But areas of training that will result in a much higher return and save police lives cannot be ignored any longer if policing is to be improved. Just as the officer spends much more of his time in interpersonal communications and needs more training in that area, all officers spend much more time eating than in shoot-don't shoot situations. Police officers desperately need more education about nutrition and diet (diet is the food that is eaten, whereas nutrition is what the food does, or does not, contain).

Training works. Officers are intelligent and they will respond to sensible, factual information presented without sensational scare tactics. Police must be educated to the real dangers of police work. Nutrition and physical fitness education must become an addition to basic recruit training. There's no purpose in "whippin'em into shape" in recruit training and then providing no classroom education or career incentive reinforcing the necessity to stay in shape.

Foreign police trained with a career orientation do not suffer the poor health affecting our police. Diet, nutrition, sleep, exercise, and attitude contribute to health and longevity. Education-training in these areas will reduce heart attacks among United States police.

Like firefighters, police spend seemingly endless hours, or even weeks, doing little that requires any physical exertion. Then suddenly the officer finds himself chasing a burglar through back yards or helping to carry a 300-pound stroke victim down two flights of stairs. The officer who is not prepared for this physically and remains in marginal or poor health is in danger of becoming another forgotten statistic. Most of these deaths are preventable with health education and incentives and encouragement from the police department. It is no secret that a healthy employee is a better employee. They are happier and they save money for the employer. It seems reasonable to conclude that a healthier officer would be a better officer.

The study of police salaries is laden with contradictions. Police salaries are hot topics for debate, but cold subjects for research. No other police subject receives more attention and less serious study. Little mention is ever made of any possible relationship between salaries and performance or production. Police frequently argue that they are underpaid in comparison to another police department, but almost never are salaries equated with task analyses or role responsibilities.

The literature review predicted a strong positive correlation between agency size and salary. The research expected to find that the more officers a police department employed, the higher the salaries would be. The perception among officers has been that the smaller the agency, the less it pays.

This research concluded that the best, single predictor variable of police department size was salary. The fewer police officers there are on a police department, the lower their annual salaries will tend to be; the larger the police department, the higher the salaries (see Appendix E). It is useless to cite specific salary figures, since they are outdated so soon.

Regional cost of living indexes and typical police lifestyles must also be considered in a serious study of police salaries. The percentage of officers on a police department, or in a particular state, that qualify (including those who qualify but do not apply) for food stamps, welfare, or other public assistance programs certainly indicates the relative inadequacy of police salaries. The ratio of police families living at or below the national poverty level also begs for attention and serious study. Almost all police officers suffering such low salaries are employed by small town or rural police departments.

A second job for a big city officer is more frequently a luxury than a survival tactic. A former student of mine now works for the Houston Police Department. His starting salary was more than what I, a university professor, was paid at the time, and he still receives a base pay greater than mine. After hours, he works less than forty hours a week at a clean, easy, palace guard type, second job and makes more money from it than from the City of Houston. Additionally, he lives in a nice, furnished apartment, rent free. The owner feels the mere presence of a police officer deters problems. In contrast, I've had several students leave small town police departments and go to larger police departments or get out of police work solely because of salary.

A second job for a small town or rural officer is usually a survival tactic. He needs the money to pay bills. So the proportion of officers on a police department, or in a region, who moonlight is not a reliable indicator of salary inadequacies.

When fringe benefits are considered, the picture becomes even more bleak. Although many larger police departments offer poor or unattractive employee benefits, a disproportionately larger number of small town and rural police departments offer very few or no benefits. Thousands of small towns and rural agencies provide no benefits of any kind to employees. Tens of thousands of small town and rural officers do not have a retirement program sponsored at least in part by the employer.

The most obvious explanation for salary disparity among different size police departments is the best one. Larger municipal governments have a stronger and greater financial base. More people means more money in the budget, which in turn means more resources to earn more money. It takes money to make money. The revenue producing machinery of a city grows exponentially as the population increases.

The best kept secret today in the world of municipal governments is the return on the investment of the police dollar. The smaller the municipality or county government, the greater will be the return on the investments in the police. Small town and rural governments have proven themselves much more adept than larger cities at turning revenues into patrol officers policing on the street. Even though smaller municipal governments are the most effective and efficient in their police operation, they lack the fiscal reserves and stability to pay adequate salaries. The greater efficiency and effectiveness of small town and rural police are discussed in more detail in another chapter.

It has been successfully argued that dumping more money into policing solves few, if any, problems and almost never improves policing. However, it must be remembered that these arguments are virtually always based on reviews of big city police operations. Such cities long ago passed the saturation point of diminishing returns. Throwing more money on the fire is a complete waste.

However, just as this maximum point exists for larger cities, a minimum subsistence point exists for small town and rural governments. Many big cities are beyond their maximum limit, and many smaller towns are below their minimum line. If police services, in any size city or county, are to be effective, satisfactory, and contemporary, then those police officers must be compensated with salaries and benefits that not only exceed the minimum subsistence amount and the national poverty level but are above the average per capita income for that state. Like education, salaries must be above, not below, public averages.

Officers earning greater salaries are usually more careful to do nothing that might jeopardize their job security. They will not risk losing their salary, not to mention the fringe benefits. They know if they lose their job, they have lost a lot. In contrast, the small town or rural police officer has little or no job security and a salary so ridiculously low that he will often lie and inflate it to an acceptable level. Clearly he really has very little to lose. He sometimes takes unnecessary or even foolish risks for the hell of it. Police officers by and large are an adventuresome lot and, without job security or a valuable salary, there's no reason not to involve oneself in fun and excitement. Perhaps if some police salaries were greater, incidents of corruption, brutality, and personnel turnover would be less.

The variables of education and salary each have a strong positive correlation to police department size. These two are also related to each other. The higher salaries of the larger agencies attract the recent college graduates. These people are willing to move before the ink has dried on their diplomas to secure an attractive salary. They do not consider styles, philosophies, or effectiveness of policing. Their major consideration is salary.

Peer pressure and tradition also play a role in their decision. Others before them have joined the larger police departments because of the salary; so it appears to be the proper course of action. Anxious to get involved in the excitement and fun of real police work and their first job, these fresh college graduates do not realize that the likelihood of their being involved in the investigation of serious cases is actually much greater on a smaller police department. They are victims of the myth that nothing exciting ever happens in small town and rural policing. Many recent college graduates starting big city police careers are lured there by the reality of higher salaries and an unreal notion of police work.

Nationwide, the most effective policing is rewarded with the lowest salaries; and the least effective policing is reinforced with the highest salaries. This practice can lead small town and rural police officers to cynicism or despair and is the primary reason many of them move to larger police departments. This negative relationship between effectiveness and salary leads to the stark realization of a very large fundamental flaw in the United States' approach to policing. Australia has hundreds of one and two-man police "stations"; yet these officers are paid on the same scale as officers working in Sydney, the largest city on the continent. Most developed countries pay police in a similar fashion.

The United States cannot have it both ways. There cannot be sweeping police innovations implemented that will have a lasting effect in the big cities, while simultaneously ignoring small town and rural police salaries. To improve the whole, each part must be improved. But to improve the status of the police occupation overall, will require considerable increases in salaries for small town and rural police.

The idea of relating police salaries to job performance is certainly a radical one, but not as premature as it first appears. Assembly-line workers in Detroit demanded and received increasingly greater wages annually for many years. Absolutely no attention was paid to work performance or product quality. The United Auto Workers (UAW) lobbied long and hard for more pay and never displayed interest in quality control. No reasonable thinking person would argue that the two should not be linked. The UAW agreed to an unprecedented pay cut only after their survival was threatened by United States citizens buying lower priced yet higher quality imports. It gives cause to wonder how low the overall quality of policing will dip before serious, long-range corrective action is taken.

Education-training, salary, and job performance are not unrelated in the police world. Any of the three can be ignored only at the expense of the others. Excessive concentration of attention on any of the three will also cause the others to suffer. Blind, unquestioned increases in police salaries will not help. Like the chef perfecting a recipe that has three major ingredients, considerable study, experimentation, time, and resources must be expended to discover the desired ratio necessary to improve our police.

Looking at how other professions have traditionally fared in small towns and rural areas produces not one single shred of hope. Country doctors, small town lawyers, and rural school teachers have always suffered lower wages than their counterparts in large cities. Unlike small town and rural police, however, they have not had to endure the slings and arrows against their reputation because of industry standards and

requirements. It is possible that low salaries are an unavoidable alba-
tross around the neck of small town and rural police. It is true that many
superb police officers spend their entire careers with small town and
rural police departments. Clearly, there is much more to staying in police work than money. Still, there are too many small town and rural police departments with salaries below the minimum subsistence level.
These are the police departments with extraordinarily high turnover
rates, and no one staying long enough to retire.

State commissions charged with overseeing police training and standards should seize the initiative and recommend minimum police salaries for their respective states. These commissions have set minimum
training and education requirements, certification standards, and
occupation-entry criteria. It would certainly not be out of order to recommend minimum pay scales. It is their duty to help improve policing.

When focusing on the larger agencies, they leave themselves open to
charges of discrimination. These state bodies have ignored two issues
too long. They must first show more sincere concern and less bureaucratic lip service in an attempt to raise the lowest salaries of small town
and rural police departments. There has been too much talk in this matter and too little action. Secondly, state police standards commissions
must squarely face the reality that policing in their state cannot be improved or professionalized as long as small town and rural officers are
slighted. To improve the whole, each part must be improved. Small
town and rural police salaries are the most rotten apples in the barrel of
police problems.

Small town and rural police officers tend to work where they live,
while officers on larger police departments tend to live where they work.
This suggests a different initial career orientation, and it encourages a
different emphasis on career orientation. Small town and rural officers
have much stronger ties to their community. They feel that they are a
part of the community both as an individual citizen and as a police officer. They are more influenced by loyalty to and group identification
with the community.

Only a very small percentage of all officers actually stumble into police work, as was believed for many years. Most officers enter police
work because it appeals to them, it is action oriented, and they possess a
genuine desire to help others. Almost all officers who leave police work
before fulfilling the requirements of a financial retirement program do
so for reasons unrelated to the size of their employing police department. But, by carefully studying those who remain in policing for a

professional career and those who leave a police department after only a few years, one can find evidence of variation in career orientation by department size.

There are thousands of men and women today working for small towns and rural police departments with a very poor or even no retirement program. With unattractive salaries and few or no financial benefits, their career orientation is frequently the only reason they remain in the job. They know they are providing a valuable service to their community and helping others. Very few officers with larger police departments would remain police officers under such circumstances. The career orientation of small town and rural officers is the force that energizes many of them to remain on the job for the duration of their productive years. They certainly don't stay on the job because of salaries and fiscal fringe benefits.

The small town or rural police officer orients his career more towards the personal, intangible, quality-of-life, human aspects of policing. Like the small town school teacher, doctor, or country lawyer, small town and rural police officers have a life first and a career second. They are satisfied with their lives; and in general they are comfortable with their careers, since their career is only a part of their total life.

Most small town and rural police officers live in the communities they police. Most police officers employed with larger police departments do not live in the areas where they police but rather live in smaller communities or surburbs. The benefits of working near home are numerous, if home happens to be located in an area not exceeding a certain population.

Studies have repeatedly shown that the majority of residents of big cities prefer to live some place else, and the majority of small town and rural residents would not move if given the opportunity. The quality of life and the perceived average lifestyle act as significant influences on the way small town and rural police officers orient their careers. Like virtually all police officers, they are loyal to policing, their careers, and their jobs; but small town and rural officers display even greater loyalties to their communities, the people in those communities, and the quality of life (see Appendix F).

If a small town or rural officer quits after only a few years of police work, he is much more likely than the officer quitting the larger police department to leave police work entirely. The small town or rural officer will probably remain in the community and secure another job. His lifestyle and environment come first and the job second. The officer with a larger police department who quits after only a few years of police work is much more likely to seek employment with another police department. His career orientation places top priority on a police career. The lifestyle and salary this officer wants will follow with another police job, he reasons. The officer working for the larger police department identifies with people in the police fraternity, in terms of career orientation, while the officer working for the smaller police department identifies more with people in the community.

This does not imply that the small town or rural officer is less conscientious. When all the evidence has been collected and analyzed, it may indicate just the opposite. Small town and rural police officers may be more conscientious than their big city counterparts. It can be argued that since the officer with the smaller police department is better known in his community than the officer in the larger city is known in his city, the small town or rural police officer feels more pressure and obligations to perform better. Other supporting evidence is suggested by the recent increased interest in organized labor movements shown by officers on larger police departments. Frequently, these movements concern only expanced job benefits and improved working conditions with little mention of performance. Coincidentally, the small town or rural officer displays a different career orientation with very limited interest in organized labor groups within the police vocation but with increasing interests in job performance and service delivery.

Any police officer who is confronted with a missing child report minutes before shift's end, even when there is no overtime pay or compensatory time, will feel a certain professional obligation to work overtime without compensation. However, because of stronger ties to the community (which give rise to additional feelings of personal obligation), the absence of a bureaucracy to handle the problem, and a sense of sacrifice found only on small town and rural police departments, the small town or rural police officer is less likely to drop the pick when the whistle blows.

Officers on big city police departments are more prone to view policing as just a job. They tend to view their position as an exchange of their time, skills, and risks for so many dollars. The small town or rural officer, in contrast, tends to view his position more in terms of personal involvement and intangible rewards. When the police occupation no longer supplies the officer on the larger police department with financial security, he will leave the occupation. When the occupation no longer fulfills personal, human, and group needs, the officer on the smaller police department will exit the occupation. What one must have, the other considers a nice luxury. What the other must have, the former considers to be a nice, but unnecessary, luxury.

Career orientations are predictable knowing the size of the police department. The bureaucracy is oriented towards the tangible: paperwork, the time clock, and the paycheck. The small group, in direct contrast, is oriented towards the intangible: personal needs, human relationships and values, and group dynamics. Consequently, the career orientation of a police officer is a reflection of the way his department views policing; which in turn is a function of the size of the police department.

Chapter 5

STRESS

JOSEPH WAMBAUGH, Eddie Donovan, Joseph McNamara, and lesser known police officers have made worthwhile progress in educating the general public about another very real but often overlooked danger of police work—stress. Nutrition, physical fitness, mental health, and stress are related.

For too long, everyone, even the police themselves, have believed officers to be dynamic, tough, strong, macho men who possessed no emotions, fears, or apprehensions. Officers were often afraid to address their own feelings and refused to express these emotions because they believed doing so would be revealing a weakness.

Policing is very stressful. The police deal constantly with people in very intense, emotional, strained situations. The burglary or theft victim can be just as emotionally upset and stressed as the battered spouse or rape victim. The officer handling these cases cannot avoid identifying to some degree with the victim. Stress is contaminating, if not contagious.

Stress is a by-product of change. The rape victim and the burglary victim have both experienced sudden, unexpected, radical changes in their lives. Some unknown person with no right to victimize others has exerted frightening control over the victim's life. The victim's realization that their life has been altered and they had no control over that change is stressful. The officer is not immune to identifying with the victim and adopting some of the same stressful reactions.

Street officers must sometimes observe the results of a human intentionally, or neglectfully, hurting a totally innocent person. The officer will develop certain defenses, a thick skin or a morbid sense of humor, to protect himself. However, such defenses are temporary at best. Time and caseload will erode the strongest armor. Added to this is the officer's own helpless feeling. The officer feels obligated to right a wrong. After all, it is the police role (or at least the officer views his role as such) to see that justice is accomplished. But the officer looks at the victim of a hit-run, drunken driver and knows that he has no control over any of this tragic circumstance.

We all experience change in our lives and some stress. Police are involved in the most trying of these experiences. Events which become the unforgettable in our entire lives are the everyday bread and butter of police work. Police officers find the concentrated and magnified human endeavors of tragedy and comedy. We expect the police to react with emotionless detachment to the very same things we will gossip, laugh, and cry about for many years to come. We expect the police to do what we cannot do, and so it follows that we sometimes expect them to do what cannot be done.

Stress is a part of every life, and it is not always unhealthy. One type of stress, *eustress* is positive, healthy, and energizes an officer. For example, another job assignment, new supervisor, or moving to a different police department can be beneficial to the officer and improve his job performance. Changes can be pleasing and still produce stress. A certain amount of eustress is desirable for optimum job performance.

Other types of stress are negative, inhibit achievement and result in health problems. They are referred to as *distress*. Many of the psychosomatic problems police suffer such as alcoholism, ulcers, nervous disorders, off-duty social dysfunctions, and suicide result from distress. The productive, happy, healthy officer maintains a balance between eustress and distress.

The ultimate experience in police work is the adrenalin rush. This is most often encountered in the field as a result of "real" police work. However, it can also result from a lengthy, complex, or monotonous investigation which ends with a favorable conclusion. It causes an increase in blood pressure, heart rate, muscle tone, and pain threshold.

Stress is divided into three stages: alarm reaction, resistance, and exhaustion. The alarm reaction is the body's immediate normal reaction to a fight or flight situation. Frequently police can do neither. Hormones and sugar are dumped into the body's biochemical system in the alarm reaction stage, exciting muscles and nerves. When the stimuli remains, the body continues to supply adrenalin even when it is no longer needed. The officer is "keyed up;" and many body functions, such as digestion, are severely disrupted.

If stress-producing stimuli remain, the body will develop a resistance to the biochemical imbalance. In the resistance stage, the officer is more in control and expends less energy in fighting emotions.

In the exhaustion stage, the effects of stress overcome the body's defenses; and many of the emotions experienced during alarm reaction return. Severe psychological and physiological problems may develop after the officer's defense mechanism has weakened or failed. Stress takes its toll in the exhaustion stage. Depending upon the duration and degree of stress, and the individual, the effects of stress range the full spectrum from slight discomfort to incapacitation to death. Stress tolerance varies from officer to officer, but the costs of stress are always significant. Many years spent in police work can shorten one's life expectancy not by days or weeks but by years.

The professional career officer who adapts and adjusts to and enjoys the unpredictable, ever-changing, exciting, action-oriented, emotion-filled world of policing will experience few problems until retirement. The adrenalin junkie must now go cold turkey. Withdrawal and total abstinence is frequently impossible. Disengagement from police work is often soon followed by attempts at reengagement. The individual will become a nuisance around the police department, join the reserves, go to work in private security, or buy a scanner. Desperately, the former officer tries to go back to yesterday. He realizes that policing is a hard act to follow. He wonders and has doubts about what remains after years of policing. He knows that policing is a participant sport although everyone else believes it to be a spectator event. After years as a police officer, is there anything else?

Hyperactivity, crying, cursing, joking, inactivity, eating, and alcohol consumption are common responses used to cope with stress. These compensations are used because stress burns stored nutrition and energy resources at a rapid rate. Stress disturbs the established delicate physical-mental balance. However, if tensions are not controlled with one of the regulators, the individual will display more advanced symptoms. The officer who yells and curses out of public sight, races down the back roads, or beats an innocent tree with his night stick, is releasing pressure. Without releases and regulators, the pressure will increase to an explosive point.

As the pressure increases, aggression escapes and the officer exhibits a need to destroy this evil. Police brutality is only one example of external aggression. Alcoholism is an example of the officer trying to maintain internal control. Those with internal controls will blame and hurt themselves, while those who have external controls will blame and hurt others.

In the most severe reactions to stress, all control is lost. The officer is out of control and he knows it. He is now the embodiment of the total contradiction. Once a decisive leader filled with confidence and always in complete control, he now finds himself filled with hopelessness and despair, completely and totally out of control. He has become what he abhorred on the street. Forever the police officer, single-handedly he will correct the problem. He destroys that which he sees but does not like. It remains simply a choice of weapons: will be put the barrel of his service revolver or the bottle of alcohol in his mouth?

As police psychologist Dr. John Stratton emphasizes, nowhere is the adage, an ounce of prevention is worth a pound of cure, more appropriate than here. Again the key is education. Officers must be educated regarding stress in their recruit training and reminded of its dangers throughout their careers.

Successful stress prevention education focuses on self awareness. The individual officer must be taught to locate individual limitations and weaknesses. Personal emotions and feelings must be addressed and accepted. The officer, who will spend a career helping others, must learn that it is a sign of strength, not weakness, to ask for help. The recruit should learn the many indicators of stress, its sources, types, and coping methods. Knowledge is strength. This initial training should be integrated with classroom education on physical fitness, exercise, and nutrition.

Many doctors state that as much as 85 percent of all illness is stress-related. Obviously, education about the triad of physical fitness, stress, and nutrition is a wise investment with long-range, high-return benefits.

Successful stress management and rehabilitation focus on peer counseling. Police are hesitant to confide in others, especially those outside the brotherhood. When officers are encouraged to unload their troubles on their peers, the results are almost always noteworthy. The keystone of the enormous universal success of Alcoholics Anonymous is peer counseling. Misery loves company. Police officers are relieved to find other officers who feel the same way; those who have survived and overcome similar or worse experiences. The brave have always been lonely; but officers must learn they can be brave and good police officers, without being lonely.

By examining different sources of stress, or *stressors,* it is easier to understand how stress affects officers and how these effects vary with department size.

The court system is perhaps the best known police stressor. An officer works hard and makes a lead-pipe case only to discover the prosecutor refuses to take it to court, or the case does make its way to court only to be disposed of prematurely for any one of many reasons. Frequently, such a case will progress all the way through the process and then result in an acquittal. In each of the examples the officer might blame himself (internal) or the system (external).

If the officer blames himself, he feels he has failed. He did not do his best. A criminal went free because the officer failed. In such situations even the strongest character cannot long survive such assaults on self esteem. In these situations the officer has expanded his presumed sphere of control to the ridiculous point of feeling responsible for something completely beyond his control.

Knowing and proving are two different things in the court system. The police officer *knows* the defendant committed the crime. The officer arrested the burglar as he crawled out the store window. The prosecutor does not prove all the elements of burglary beyond a reasonable doubt, and the burglar walks out of the courtroom a free man. The system presumes the suspect is innocent until proven guilty. Again, the officer harbors a contradiction. It seems the burglar is guilty and innocent. The officer attempts to reconcile this by interpreting the court's verdict as an affront on his integrity. Since his integrity is all he has, the officer feels the system is attacking him.

If the officer blames the court system, then he is likely to adopt the attitude: "What's the use? The court will just turn them loose." Both situations are extreme, stressful, and inaccurate. The officer needs to be educated to the reality of court bureaucracy. The officer uses one standard which is proper while the court looks at the same case in a different light, which is also proper. The prosecutor chooses not to prosecute for any of a number of reasons. The officer can reduce stress in this area by understanding that he is only one of several key players in the process, and a refusal to prosecute or an acquittal may simply indicate that other key players are conscientiously pursuing their roles. The wise officer understands the adversarial process but is very careful not to incorporate it into his own personality. The wise officer controls stress by recognizing that the court system, like policing, is a compromise. Not all criminals are convicted, but many are. Not all offenders are arrested, but many are.

Small town and rural police sometimes have a slight advantage because of their closer, more personal relationship with the prosecutor. In a few cases the prosecutor will feel more obligated to take a case to court because he knows the officer. In other cases the prosecutor does not take the case to court, but he or an assistant will spend considerable time with the officer explaining why.

Community attitudes can be a stressor for some officers. When the relationship between the police and the policed is strained or lacking in respect, the individual officer is certainly in a more hostile and stressful atmosphere. The small town and rural police officer is more likely to work in a community where the public and the police are less likely to be at odds. The probability of the police and the public, therefore, having mutual respect is much greater in small town and rural areas. Consequently, small town and rural police encounter stress induced by negative or unfavorable community attitudes less frequently.

Ineffective referral agencies can be a stressor for police officers in the larger cities and small towns near metropolitan areas. For example, when a citizen tells an officer that an agency to which the police previously referred the citizen failed to provide services, the officer may accept the blame. However, rural police and many small town officers have few or no referral services available. What might be a detriment to the citizen is in this case a benefit to the officer. Ineffective referral services are just one more price that must be paid for a large bureaucracy. The emphasis is clearly on efficiency, not effectiveness, or the idea of referrals.

On larger police departments the bureaucracy itself is a major source of stress. The cold, remote, impersonal, uncaring hallmarks of a bureaucracy are the antithesis of everything that makes an effective, conscientious officer. The police department is telling the officer that he must avoid treating people the way the police department treats people. Do as I say, not as I do. There is no doubt why many big city officers are impersonal and bureaucratic in their dealing with people.

Just as the police officer is the most visible representative of the establishment to many citizens, the sergeant is the most visible representative of the bureaucracy to the big city officer. The bureaucracy is invisible while the immediate supervisor is an easy target. On larger police departments the sergeant is the leading cause of stress in the eyes of the officers.

Police work demands that officers possess certain characteristics such as initiative, decisiveness, courage, good judgement, and other traits of leadership. An officer must be a leader. Sometimes he observes what he believes is a flaw or incompetence in his supervisor. This is stressful because it affects him, but he perceives himself as having no control over it. Good leaders are not always good followers.

In larger police departments first line supervisors cause stress in two ways. They are stressors because they have the very difficult job of leading leaders, and because they are the embodiment of the bureaucracy. The sergeant might also be unfitted for a supervision position. He might be a superb officer, and a total failure as a police supervisor. *The Peter Principle* (a person rises to his level of incompetence) works as well in a larger police department as in any other bureaucracy. Since officers are cloaked in authority, it is not uncommon to find a sergeant on a power trip. Perhaps he has lost his orientation to authority with the stripes; perhaps he never had a healthy orientation. Larger police departments can help all their officers by providing the proper screening and training of potential supervisors.

Some officers are attracted to the supervisor's job solely because it means an increase in pay. This indicates that the department has failed to provide adequate career development opportunities. The best police officers on a police department should be on the street policing, and the best supervisors should be supervising. More career paths must be made available for the patrol officer. It should be an honor, not a disgrace, to spend an entire police career as a patrol officer. This would eliminate considerable pressure on the officer to seek promotion and would eliminate a lot of unnecessary stress.

Limited opportunity is a major stressor for small town and rural police. Many of these officers cannot accept the complete absence of any possibility of any rank or salary increase. Not all small town and rural officers are faced with such dismal prospects, but a disproportionate large number are. Small town and rural police departments do not have the ratio of ranking and supervisory positions of larger police departments. It comes with the territory. Many of these officers recognize it will be many years before any openings develop, and perhaps opportunities will not develop in twenty or more years.

Reward and recognition is probably weak or absent more often in larger groups than in smaller, more personal groups. The most meaningful recognition to police officers comes from their peers. A sincere handshake, a wink, good-natured kidding, or even locker room banter, when properly delivered, are all forms of reinforcement which every officer needs and appreciates. Unfortunately for those working for larger police departments, this is too often neglected or forgotten in the day-to-day operations of a bureaucracy.

Police officers are of above average intelligence. They also develop a sense of humor to cope with the stress of the job. The combination of above average intelligence and a finely honed sense of humor often produces interesting and important results. Sergeant A worked on a police department of about 200 officers. He was a superb police officer, admired and respected by all, truly a man for all seasons. Sergeant B worked for the same police department. He had been a complete failure as a street officer and had proven himself to be an incompetent supervisor. Born unlikeable he became the quintessence of a jerk. A small group of officers conspired for weeks to stage a surprise birthday party for Sergeant A. Covert operations were elaborate. All evidence trails had to be erased. The day of the big job finally arrived. During the evening shift change, a large expensive cake with personalized icing appeared out of nowhere. Sergeant B happened to be there also. Dozens of officers joined in singing happy birthday to Sergeant A. There was even punch and a present or two. In response to the usual demands for a speech, Sergeant A rose and spoke with modesty. He thanked everyone, admitted surprise, and made a brief remark about the camaraderie. He then dropped a bombshell: it was not his birthday, not even close. Everyone appeared startled and perplexed. But by then, it was time to hit the street and go to work. The unenlightened outsider would never understand; it was Sergeant B's birthday.

It was great fun. One of those involved did not learn until many years later in graduate school that this helped in coping with stress. It also served an important purpose of communicating to both supervisors precisely what the group thought of each. Ironically, in the macho world of policing, it was far easier to communicate verbally one's candid feelings to Sergeant B than to Sergeant A. Police courage makes it easy to critize, complain, and condemn. Police conventionality makes it difficult to express one's warm, personal side. A balance is healthy and desirable.

Many small town and rural police departments have no written policy. This can produce considerable stress. The officer knows that no matter how he handles a case, the chief can always accuse him of using poor judgement. Police work then is no longer a judgement call, but merely the flip of a coin. Officers on police departments with a thousand or more people suffer a very similar stress. They have written policy, but it is frequently written in such a vague way as to leave interpretation up to the whims of the chief. "The officer will always use good judgement and do nothing that might discredit the department." "The officer will use discretion consistent with tradition and professional police practices." Heads the chief wins, tails the officer loses.

Excessive paperwork produces stress for many officers. This stressor seems a good example of how great a role an officer's perception of stress plays in his reaction to a stressor. Some officers wade through tons of paperwork, year after year, with no problems whatsoever. Another officer, same police department, same shift, adjacent beat, appears overwhelmed with only a relatively few reports. Individual perception plays a major role in stress. What stresses one officer to the breaking point might prove boring to another. Stress is still stress, however, and it must be addressed and treated no matter when or where it is found. To be forewarned is to be forearmed. The recruit in the academy must be alerted to the many known stressors so that he can watch for and locate his own.

Alienation produces stress for anyone. The "us versus them" attitude found on some larger police departments separates the officer from his community. This stress is dangerous because it spreads insidiously in the individual and the group. It is a barrier to effective policing because police who are adversaries with their communities are not police.

Alienation is found less often on the small town and rural police department. The officer has stronger and closer support groups. Family, church, neighbors, childhood friends, longtime acquaintances, and others all function as stress release valves.

The absence of closure is a significant stressor for many big city officers, but not for small town and rural police. In the larger department the officer makes an arrest or deals with a victim and frequently never learns the outcome of his cases. In the small town the officer often follows up on cases because he is interested and because he considers it part of his job. He knows this person, victim or suspect, and knows he will probably have occasion to deal with them again. It helps the officer maintain a perspective much more closely aligned with reality.

The larger city officer usually must go out of his way to learn the outcome of a case. The small town or rural officer usually learns the outcome of a case as a part of the normal course of events. The person working for a police department with fewer than sixteen officers in a large metropolitan area will most likely experience less closure and more stress.

Other researchers examined police stress and its implications. Sandy and Devine isolated four factors that appeared to be unique to rural policing: security, social factors, working conditions, and inactivity.

One aspect of security remains the number of officers available to respond to a given situation. The officer working without a backup officer may frequently find himself in a dangerous position. Police science, his training, experience, and judgement, all tell him that he needs a back-up. Reality denies him that which he knows he should have. The officer finds himself in a situation which, because of no backup, is perceived as more dangerous than it should be. Having no control over this added degree of danger, the officer is distressed. When the small town or rural officer lives with no hope of things improving in the foreseeable future, the effects of this distress can be cumulative.

This may explain some incidents of police brutality on small town or rural police departments. The officer suffers the pressure of stress, and at the first opportunity the officer will display the control which remained checked in all the cases without a backup. Control is demonstrated by over-reacting and using unnecessary force. This officer reassures the world in general and himself in particular that he is in control, and he has the power and force to maintain control.

Another aspect of security stressors is the prevalence of firearms in rural homes. Rural officers frequently have the perception that virtually all rural households have at least one firearm. Although such perceptions are invariably based on anecdotal information, it matters little since the officer's attitude will be based on perceptions, not reality; and attitude is a major determinate of stress. All of the officer's training and experience has underscored the danger of firearms. Again the officer is confronted with an added degree of danger, and the officer realizes he has no control over this increased danger.

One of the greatest concerns and fears of all officers is whether or not this particular individual is armed. Once the officer can see the person's hands or is otherwise satisfied that the risk is minimum, then the officer can proceed with some confidence. The game warden or rural officer, in contrast, often assumes that the other party is armed and always proceeds with caution.

These two stressors, no backup and the common occurence of firearms, can serve as a super-stressor when they are combined, which is often in small town and rural policing.

Social factors account for both eustress and distress. In small town and rural police work there is often an absence of anonymity. Although this is a key to effective policing and one of the major differences between small and large police departments, it can be a source of distress for the individual officer. The officer is perceived by himself and the community as a police figure at all times. He is unable to assume any role in social endeavors other than that of an officer. This infringes on his personal relationships, many of which were well established before

he joined the police department. On a larger police department the officer seeks out and establishes new social contacts within the police department. This is usually impossible for the officers working for a police
department with fewer than ten or twelve officers.

However, these stressors are unique to small town and rural occupations and not just small town and rural police. Small town public school
teachers, for example, endure some of the same distress. The community expects them to behave within certain parameters. To lose their professional identity they must go to a larger city where they are unknown.
Officers with larger police departments can enjoy their "choir practices"
or "library meetings" without notice in any bar hidden in the urban
mass. Officers with smaller police departments do not enjoy such benefits. They must wait, like the small town school teacher or dentist, for an
out-of-town training session or convention to kick up their heels and let
down their hair.

For the small town or rural sheriff, chief, or top level administrator,
this problem becomes more exaggerated. He finds himself with no support group and few or no confidants. The patrol officer has few peers;
the administrator has none.

In a hostile or arrestable confrontational situation, the small town or
rural police officer is much more likely to find himself face to face with a
friend or acquaintance of many years. The decision to arrest can be distressful by itself. With the added strain of testing personal relationships
and loyalties, this police situation can be most stressful. This is not an
infrequent dilemma in small town and rural policing. If the officer
makes the arrest he takes the risk not only of severing that social relationship but of losing other contacts as well. If the officer does not make
the arrest, he takes the risk not only of being critized for not doing his
job but of losing some self respect as well.

Stressors in working conditions include salaries, promotions, and
fringe benefit packages. The small town or rural officer who never
compares his salary to that paid by a larger police department is extremely rare. Sometimes he does not understand the economic reality
underlying such an obvious disparity. He knows he is performing essentially the same function, but yet he feels he is underpaid by comparison. He compares promotional opportunities in the same manner.
He rationalizes that he has no alternative but to conclude that he has
failed; he is not as good an officer as the person working for the larger
police department. Such an attitude is distressful and often leads
directly to depression.

Inactivity has been listed as a stressor that is unique to small town and rural police. In all probability this is nothing more than another myth about how police departments vary by size. Officers on all size police departments are subject to experiencing long spells of inactivity. That is the very nature of police work. It is always unpredictable, either feast or famine. The officer frequently has either nothing to do, or he has so much to do that it is impossible to do it all. Long periods of inactivity may be much more common in a particular social type of community, but the size of the police department has never been shown to have any relationship to the amount or duration of police inactivity.

The amount of police inactivity, like policing itself, varies with the social composition of the community, the police philosophy and style of the police department and the individual officer, and the expectations of the policed population. It does not vary because of the size of the police department. Television has misled many into the belief that big city officers are always busy in exciting roles and small town and rural officers are always inactive in static, predictable, lackluster positions. A look at reality indicates otherwise.

It has already been established, however, that an officer's perception plays a larger role in stress than reality. Expectations also play a significant role in stress. Officers who expect policing efforts to result in obvious improvements in the community and public safety environment expect a lot and will be disappointed. Expecting too much out of policing causes stress. If the small town or rural police officer perceives his role as a police officer to be that of the action-packed, nonstop big city officer, his expectations will probably remain unfulfilled, as will the same expectations by big city officers. The officer on any size department who expects policing to be predictable, routine, or consistent in any way will suffer the stress of unrealized expectations. Their perceptions and expectations are too far removed from reality for these officers to enjoy a happy, healthy, distress-free police career.

During training police recruits must be presented with an accurate picture of policing in their jurisdiction if they are to ever develop into successful officers. Anything that is said or done which can be easily misinterpreted will produce unrealistic expectations. Later, when the officer's experiences and observations do not match those expectations, the stress reaction will manifest itself as cynicism.

Cynicism has been tolerated and even nourished for so long in some police circles that it has become a part of the police culture in many regions of the country. One study found that chiefs of smaller police departments were more cynical than chiefs of larger police departments. Several explanations exist to help understand this. It is a common practice for officers with many years service on a larger police department to retire to a small town as chief. The fact that this career officer was overly cynical might help explain the reason he never advanced into the executive ranks in the larger police department.

If a chief or high ranking administrator on any police department is frozen in stagnation by excessive cynicism, all those below him will be adversely affected. Stress disguised as cynicism has probably prevented more good police work and promoted more bad police community relations than any other single factor in the history of policing. The contagiousness and danger of cynicism cannot be overstated. On many police departments cynicism is an accepted and expected form of behavior. Recruits fresh out of the academy on these police departments adopt a cynical attitude for no reason except that it insures their acceptance into the clique.

Stress and cynicism are coconspirators. To attack one and ignore the other is self-defeating. Hearing excessive cynicism from one's peers is likely to produce stress in the conscientious officer, and stress often finds an acceptable outlet in cynicism. Cynicism becomes excessive when it affects police community relations, or when it adversely affects job performance. Like prejudices, cynical thoughts must remain the officer's most closely guarded secrets. Once they are expressed, the danger arises that the officer's relationships and performance will be discriminating. The best and safest approach is an attitude free of cynicism.

Successful and effective police officers and administrators have always been, almost without exception, those who displayed little or no cynicism. Permitting cynicism to grow until it affects performance indicates that there are no safeguards in place against stress. Possibly, this reflects poorly on the individual officer or the chief, but the results are the same. The malignancy of cynicism must be stopped because it is always a barrier to effective policing.

Stress in its many different forms remains the greatest unrecognized enemy of modern policing. It has wrecked thousands of careers, ruined and even destroyed lives, and it is an absolute impediment to effective policing. Stress can prevent effective policing at the individual officer's level, at the squad or shift level, and at the department level. In a police organization stress cripples its victim and everyone below that victim in the organization. Stress is a progressive disease that can consume one officer, many, or an entire police department if it is permitted to grow unchecked.

Police leadership must seize the initiative and arrest any further harmful effects of stress. Their best ally is training and education of officers. Powerful visionary police leadership coupled with modern scientific training can control and eliminate the disastorous effects of police stress. Intelligent, conscientious police leaders have recognized the seriousness of the threat of stress and are currently developing and implementing programs to overcome it. They realize that stress must be overcome before a community can realize and enjoy the many favorable benefits of effective policing.

Part III

DIFFERENCES IN POLICING
BY DEPARTMENT SIZE

Chapter 6

POLICE COMMUNITY RELATIONS

THE ONLY major difference between what small town and rural police do and what all other police do is found in police community relations. However, since police community relations comprises at least 90 percent of the police function, this lone difference remains profound.

Police community relations is not a certain quantity or quality of interaction between the police and the community, but rather it is any social intercourse between the police and the community. Ideally, police community relations is constant, near perfect, communication and interaction between members of the police department and members of the community. Police jargon assumes that anytime the term is used it means desirable, or good, police community relations, unless otherwise noted.

Police community relations is necessary for effective policing. The only valid and reliable measure of police effectiveness remains community satisfaction. Too frequently attempts to measure police effectiveness focus on the police. To accurately measure police effectiveness, more attention must be paid in the future to what the community wants and receives in police services.

Without a clear understanding of what the citizenry expects, the police must guess, use trial and error (which in policing always results in many trials and countless errors), or, as most often occurs, they impose the services which they believe to be best for the community. This is analogous to a medical doctor examining a patient without any form of communication between the two and then prescribing a treatment plan. Occasionally this will work, as in the case of the auto accident victim with a compound fracture of the leg. Usually, such an approach proves disastrous. The absolute necessity of communication has been well documented. It is well known to all except, importantly, many police officers and administrators.

Communication is a two-way street, but it can be initiated by either the officer or the citizen. Since the officer is in uniform, and obviously different from everyone else, the citizen is often hesitant to converse with the officer as readily and freely as with another citizen. For many reasons the officer also is reluctant to engage in idle conversation. Too frequently the officer has been trained and conditioned to perceive his role and function as not including friendly, nonbusiness interaction. The effective street officer has always known that the key to effective street policing is talk. He talks to people and listens to them talk.

In larger cities it is difficult and even sometimes taboo to initiate small talk with strangers or those outside one's immediate world. In smaller communities friendliness is the expected norm. The resident of the larger city who engages the patrol officer in small talk is violating a social norm and will be viewed with a suspicious eye by the police and citizens alike. The resident of the small town or rural area who chats with a police officer violates no community expectations and only reinforces those concepts which give the small town spirit its uniqueness.

Virtually all police officers are keenly aware of interpersonal communications as a prerequisite to effective policing. Unfortunately for policing, the majority of officers are employed by police departments that are bureaucracies. Herein lies another of the many contradictions of police work. The officer with the big city police department is in a dilemma. His better judgement tells him to be loyal to his employer and be a bureaucrat, and at the same time his better judgement tells him to be loyal to policing and be personal. He cannot do both, and he knows there is no compromise.

The police administrator in the large city is removed from the people in the community too often and becomes lost in the bureaucracy. He is preoccupied with running the bureaucracy and loses sight of the goal of policing. However, since the administrators give direction and dictate policy and procedures, the police department itself pursues the goals and objectives of a bureaucracy at the cost of ignoring the pursuit of improved police services. Perpetuation of the bureaucracy becomes more important than community relations. The superstructure rushes blindly forward without a solid foundation.

Most big city police community relations programs are nothing more than public relations. They serve only to convince the public that their local police are doing something with their tax dollars. Generally they do not accomplish their goal of improving communications between the public and the police. The very fact that the leadership on a police department chooses to establish a special section, group, or program and label it Police Community Relations, indicates that the administration is either unaware of, or is ignoring, the concept that police community relations begins and ends with the patrol officer on the beat.

The individual patrol officer in the field is the best, the only, and the total police community relations program. It is the work-a-day foot soldier who will make or destroy the image of the police department. It is the officer on the beat who totally controls the reputation of that police department, and to some degree, the reputation of all police. In police community relations, as in many other human endeavors, "The credit belongs to the man who is actually in the arena, whose face is marred by dust and sweat and blood. . . ." Continuing the analogy, the typical bureaucratic police administrator then is nothing more than "those cold timid souls who know neither victory or defeat."

The individual citizen is unlikely to respond in any favorable way to an encounter with an impersonal bureaucracy. The officer who has been programmed by a bureaucracy to perform in a military, predictable, uniform manner is very likely to deliver bureaucratic services. When humans call for police help, they want human, not bureaucratic, services. It matters little if their call for help involves a theft, a rape, the proverbial cat in the tree, or a burst kitchen sink pipe that is flooding the house, they want somebody to help them. They will not call a hospital, a plumbing company, a lawyer's office, a bank, or the fire department because they know better than to expect quick help from a bureaucracy, and because they cannot afford it. They call the police because they want and need people to help, and they believe the police will fulfill their needs by delivering certain personal, human services. Big city police administrators tend to have lost sight of these police fundamentals, and very seldom pay any serious attention to them.

Small town and rural police administrators and officers will usually lose their job if they lose sight of these same basics. Whether these officers realize what they are doing and why doesn't really matter. It's impossible to argue with success. Police community relations is the only area where small town and rural police have a great advantage. The kind of police community relations practiced by small town and rural police departments is not, as they would have us believe, a result of special skills, education, knowledge, or attitudes which they possess. Instead, this social interaction and interpersonal communication is a result and function of the small town, small group, personal attitude, concept—the small town philosophy.

I was taught in the Berkeley, California, Police Department that a community receives the kind of policing it wants. My subsequent police experiences with other police departments in other states did nothing to refute this. Numerous writers and scholars have repeated this adage with the observation that every police department is a child of, or a reflection of, the citizens it serves. The small town or rural police department is a vital, integral part of the community it serves, regardless of the number of people on the police department or the number of people in the community. The big city police department, in contrast, is an independent, self-sustaining bureaucracy.

Big cities are made of many small communities; but, unfortunately for the vast majority, they are all forced to rely on one, bureaucratic, cold police department. The citizen calling for police help will most probably never see the responding officer again, and both the citizen and the officer know that. The citizen finds it easy to view the officer as just another impersonal bureaucrat, and the officer finds it equally easy to view the citizen as just another obnoxious nuisance passing in review on the assembly line.

The small community with its own police department, surrounded by a metroplex area, would be an exception only if the overwhelming majority of its residents have adopted and practice the small town philosophy. This is what a few brave police administrators in some larger cities are trying to do with decentralization and store-front police stations. They hope function will follow form. They hope that if they copy the mechanics of the small town and rural police department, the results — improved police community relations and then improved policing — will follow.

If the desireable police community relations of small town and rural police is a function of the small town philosophy, then a thorough understanding of the latter is necessary to understand the former. Some of the major distinguishing characteristics of the small town philosophy are obvious and common knowledge, while others are not as well known. The reader must also remember that it is this philosophy, attitude, and spirit, not the population count, which defines the small town.

In Small Town, United States the individual feels a stronger bonding with the community. Even the new arrival frequently senses a feeling of belonging. Although the new kid on the block is noticed quicker and viewed with a careful inspecting eye, that person is also accepted into the community much more readily. There is a greater sense of unity in small towns than exists in big towns. The social interaction and ties, the very glue that makes us social animals and not a collection of hermits, are much more prevalent in a small town or rural community. Whether they particularly want to or not, people have a feeling of belonging in small towns.

Anomie, a condition of normlessness or the absence of standards of behavior, appears much less often in small towns than in large cities. Both formal and informal rules of behavior are more likely to be unclear, in conflict with each other, or completely absent, in the big city. Scores of explanations have been offered for big cities having significantly higher rates of delinquency, crime, and suicide. Yet, seldom is the most logical reason, anomie, mentioned.

The formal and informal standards of behavior are not only clearly defined in the small town, but very strictly enforced. Everyone knows what the community will and will not tolerate. Everyone knows what he may or may not do without the wrath of community scorn and perhaps ostracism. Rules governing every conceivable form of human behavior and deviance are generally clear in the small town. Ironically, the informal rules are the most powerful. They frequently dictate the effect of the formal ones. In big cities only the formal rules, the laws and ordinances, can be enforced. In small towns only the informal rules can be enforced. Fortunately, the informal rules of small town life include many of the laws, but only the informal standards and expectations are truly effective.

In small towns a larger percentage of the population feels a sense of purpose. They believe they are making progress toward their goals. These small town residents believe their community leaders are concerned, at least to some degree, about their community. Small town residents are more likely to believe their lives and their neighbors' lives have at least a minimum amount of order and predictability. They view their friends, neighbors, and police as dependable sources of support.

Small town gossip is a common term, whereas the term big city gossip is virtually unknown. Small town gossip serves a vital role in bonding, unifying, and reinforcing formal and informal behavior standards. Small town gossip is what all police refer to as intelligence. It is difficult for the police of larger cities to acquire intelligence because such a small percentage of the population is privy to it and because usually no one on the police department has access to it. Small town and rural police gain intelligence with ease because a comparatively large percentage of the population possess it and because usually at least one member of the police department has been exposed to it.

Esprit de corps has a tendency not only to be higher in small towns but also is of a more geniune nature. New Yorkers are rightfully proud of their city, but Small Towners are more consistent and enduring with their boasts. The relative percentage of Small Towners who are self-appointed ambassadors is far greater. The New Yorker who boasts about his/her home in the South Bronx or a particular location by street name in East Harlem is more Small Towner than New Yorker. The lifelong resident of Cody, Wyoming who extols life in Cody, is doing the very same thing for the very same reason. However, differences in both quantity and quality of communication and interaction between the average Cody resident and their police compared to New York City counterparts are enormous. Esprit de corps gives the individual one more reason to strive.

The absence of many of the unavoidable, inherent complexities of larger cities contributes in a positive way to small town magic. Seldom will more than two or three interests be involved in any one issue of small town city government. Seldom will less than five or six separate interests be involved in any one issue of big town city government. The absence of a mammoth bureaucracy insures a less frenzied pace for the police as well as all other city officials and employees. One of the basic obligations of any government is to set the tone and mood, or morale, for those governed.

Simply because of the size of small towns, the average small town resident will know a larger percentage of people in the town. Sales persons have long used a rule of 250. The customer, or person, knows on the average 250 other people. Therefore, a customer, satisfied or dissatisfied, has the potential to influence 250 other prospects. If the average person knows 250 other people, the small town resident will be familiar with a larger percentage of his home town than will the resident of the larger city. This also contributes to bonding and a general feeling of belonging. Conversely, the relative percentage of strangers is significantly less in small towns and rural communities. This has important implications for the police.

Small town and rural police are much more likely to know, or know of, individuals involved in police cases. They are also much more likely to have some future contact or reminder of such individuals. Many of us have grown so accustomed to thinking of policing with a good-guys versus bad-guys mind set that it is very difficult to understand the give and take interplay that constantly occurs between small town and rural police officers and some of their contacts. Small town and rural police for the most part accept the fact that they live in the same community as the hard core criminals and people on the fringes of crime, with whom they must frequently interact. The officer who arrests the local grocer for drunken driving will be buying groceries from him the next week, and perhaps only three people will ever know the name of the woman with the grocer when he was arrested. This knowledge is power to the small town or rural police officer, but it remains practically worthless in a larger city. In school the children of small town and rural police sit beside the children of known thieves and convicted crooks. Yet, the children interact with little or no recognition of the obvious.

In the small town philosophy, every part is crucial to the whole. No part is dispensable. The small town or rural police department is considered to be vital; the town could not exist without it. Citizens feel like they have a vested interest in their small town and in their police department. In larger cities residents frequently feel at odds with the city or the police department. You can't fight city hall. Some express the opinion that one should support your local police. In smaller cities residents sometimes feel at odds with the world outside their hometown. Big brother (the state or federal government) is trying to tell us how to run our lives. Many express the opinion that one should support our local police. An us versus them mind set exists in both settings. In the big town it's groups or individuals against each other; in the small town it's locals against outsiders. In the big town it's residents against each other; in the small town it's residents for each other.

A bumper sticker proclaiming "Everybody's somebody in Luckenbach, Texas" contains more than a hint of truth. In a community with a strong small town philosophy, everybody does sense that he plays an important role. Again, nothing more complicated than simple mathematics is required to explain this. A resident of a city of 20,000 is 1/20,000ths of that city, but a resident of a city of two million is only 1/2,000,000ths of that city. The same concept applies to police officers and will be discussed at much greater length in a later chapter. If you are an officer on a police department that has two police officers, then you are 50 percent of that police department. This instills a completely different feeling than if you were an officer on a police department of 1,200 officers. There is much more involved here than novel twisting of compared percentages.

Psychology and sociology help explain how important an individual's sense of belonging is to the health and welfare of both the group and the individual. One's sense of belonging and importance is directly related to self-esteem. A person who likes himself and is comfortable with who he is, seems much more likely to be a happy, well-adjusted group member. Certainly this contributes more than previously recognized to the higher rates of violence and violent crime in the larger cities. For example, there has always been a strong positive correlation between the population of a city and its robbery rate. Maybe in a big city, the robbers are trying to be somebody.

In Small Town, United States the individual believes that the support systems are stronger and more reliable. In Big City, United States the individual is given ample reason to lose faith in the support systems, feeling they are not as strong as necessary. Such support systems include the family, relatives, neighbors, schools, churches, service clubs and organizations, work peers, special interest groups, and social groups of various functions. If an individual is dealt a serious, stressful blow, such as losing a job, spouse, or child, or is arrested and jailed, the rate of and success of recovery is dependent to a large degree on the support systems.

Since these support systems are stronger and in closer proximity to the individual in small towns and rural communities, the damage the individual suffers will be significantly reduced. The individual, for example, who loses his job in a big metroplex is pretty much dependent on the bureaucracy to help him find another one. That person will probably spend many days waiting in line at the employment office. In contrast, when an individual in a small town loses his job, the support systems go on full alert mode, and usually it is only a matter of time until that person is working again. Even the homeless, the unemployables, the borderline mentally retarded, and all others who are less than productive, contributing members are better protected and cared for by the small town philosophy because of these stronger support systems.

When tragedy or a great personal stressor strikes in a larger city, it always seems to happen to someone else, someone the individual does not know. Sure, the big city newspapers are full of violence, crime, and despair; but the reader seldom knows the victim. One finds it easy not to identify with the suffering. In a small town or rural community, just the opposite is true. When anyone suffers, the word spreads quickly. Virtually everyone knows the victim, knows someone who knows the victim, or identifies in some way, no matter how remote, with the victim. The small town resident finds it difficult not to identify with the suffering. Perhaps some small bit of primordial survival instinct is involved. Perhaps the small town resident understands much better than the resident of the large city just how vunerable the individual really is. Perhaps the small town resident understands better how very close he came to being the victim. The big city bureaucracy has a way of insulating the individual from the worst of life.

In small towns and rural communities it appears that a larger percentage of the people are geniunely concerned about the well-being of their fellow community members. Just as the impersonal aloofness of the big city bureaucracy is frequently reflected in police services, the personal, sincere concern for others in the small town philosophy is reflected in the services provided by the police. When this occurs it is usually not because of the individual officer involved or the attitude of the police chief, but it is more directly a result of the attitude of the larger group, the populace.

Chapter 7

COMMUNITY BASED POLICING

THE ONLY major difference between small town and rural policing and all other policing consists of police community relations. However, since the vast majority of all policing involves some form of police community relations, that makes small town and rural policing profoundly different. This difference involves not so much a different police philosophy or style as it does the small town philosophy. This difference becomes more apparent by looking at the different styles and methods of policing. Small town philosophy and police community relations explain the why of the difference; *community-based policing* explains the how of the difference. Small town philosophy is the cause, police community relations the bridge, and community-based policing the effect.

Community-based policing correlates strongly with the small town philosophy. In its most oversimplified form, community-based policing is self-policing. After a group or community grows beyond a certain number, an invisible social organization, called a *bureaucracy,* emerges. The bureaucracy contains many advantages. It assumes many of the responsibilities formerly left to the individual, and thus frees the individual for other pursuits. The bureaucracy assumes the responsibility for policing. Since people no longer police themselves, they view the government as totally responsible for policing. Policing becomes someone else's job. Individuals no longer concern themselves with policing.

To examine one aspect of this idea, a review of personnel records of the inmates of any jail or prison will reveal a remarkable absence of certain minority, or small groups. Jews and Orientals reflect two of the minority groups which are proportionally underrepresented in the incarcerated population. The explanation can be none other than the fact that these people police themselves. Small town and rural areas produce thousands of convicted criminals. However, it is certainly safe and logical to hypothesize that small town and rural residents are also relatively underrepresented in the more than half a million convicted prisoners. The explanation appears the same. In the absence of a big brother bureaucracy to care for individuals, small town and rural communities care for their own. They police themselves.

Community-based policing includes many different aspects. A fugitive concept — it escapes objective definition. Community-based policing bursts forth in a few big cities as a collection of programs, ideas, and experiments. Frequently described in these big cities as innovative, progressive, promising, or an improvement, community-based policing in a big city always means one thing for sure, change in police community relations. In cities and communities which subscribe to a small town philosophy, the police and citizens know nothing but community-based policing. Implicit in the term, it does not mean big city-based policing but policing rooted in the community.

To better understand community-based policing, one must have an introduction to some of the police jargon. In 1968 James Q. Wilson studied one police department and found three types or styles of policing: *watchman, legalistic,* and *service.* Other police writers and scholars have since generalized and applied these three styles to all police officers and police departments. Many police thinkers assume that officers' behavior and police departments fit neatly into one of the three.

The watchman style of policing emphasizes maintaining the peace, keeping order, and generally maintaining the status quo. Here exists almost a total absence of law enforcement priority. These officers reason that it is better to be seen and not heard. Do not make waves. Making many arrests means many problems, few arrests means few problems, and no arrests should result in no problems. Other watchman style officers reason further, it is best not to be seen or heard. A nationally known police chief told my class that the public cannot hit a target which they cannot see. The watchman style of policing includes in part the simplistic reasoning that if the police do nothing, the public cannot and will not critize them. These include the peace officers, palace guards, and gate keepers. Unquestionably, they exist on police departments of every size serving cities of every nature. Some police departments consists predominately of officers practicing the watchman style of policing; and, therefore, that police department reflects a watchman style police department. In most such situations the community demanded, in one way or another, this type of police department.

The legalistic style of policing places great emphasis on law enforcement. The police explain, "We don't make the laws, we just enforce them." In a forced choice situation, this officer makes an arrest rather than maintain order. Since this style of policing holds the potential for action and excitement and the adrenalin rush, it attracts officers with a particular personality. They see themselves as law enforcement officers. Usually they know all the minutiae of city ordinances, the traffic code, and valid but unenforced laws still on the books. This officer practices discretion only when circumstances force him into a nonlegalistic alternative. Officers judge themselves by the number of tickets written and arrest made. Administrators reason that the officer doing his job will receive citizens' complaints, and the officer who receives no complaints does no policing. Their peers frequently refer to these officers as gung-ho, super sleuths, or hot dogs. Superb legalistic examples work on many police departments, regardless of the size of the police department or the chemistry of the community.

Two schools of thought exist in terms of a single police role in our society; and, in their extremes both appear clear and distinct. One position argues that the individual's rights must take precedence over the rights of society (the group): we must preserve order with law. The other position assumes that society's rights come before the rights of the individual: we must maintain law and order. An irresistible temptation causes many to plug the two policing styles, watchman and legalistic, into this dichotomy.

Finally, the service style of policing happens as something of a compromise between the first two, with an added concern for providing a service to the public. Officers or police departments subscribing to the service style of policing feel sensitive to the public's needs and desires. Police try pleasing all. Perhaps more realistic and appropriate in many communities than either of the other two, extreme examples of service style policing exist in all size police departments. The longest tenured chiefs include those who can best read the tea leaves of the community's wants, anticipate the winds of change, and deliver those desired police services. Likewise, a 24-carat, hot-dog officer will not feel at home on a police department that devoutly practices only service-style policing.

In addition to these three styles of policing, two philosophies of police science evolved. *Reactive* and *proactive* policing exemplify most policing philosophies.

Because a small minority of police departments employ a large majority of the officers, reactive policing occurs as the most common form of policing today, as in the past. As its name implies, reactive policing means responding to requests from the community for police assistance. Like yesterday's firefighter, this attitude requires that the police do absolutely nothing until a call for help arrives. Reactive policing promotes no creativity or originality, suggesting that police are primarily clerks and report takers. Initiative serves no purpose. Reactive policing is addictive, contagious, and ineffective. It is far easier to ride around in an air conditioned car than to get out, walk around, talk with people, and look for problem areas. Sitting in a car, people-watching, appeals more than policing to these officers. The impossibility of policing from inside a car presents a problem. The automobile gave police a tool, not a crutch. If the person with the uniform, badge, and gun expects to police, he must exit the car and enter the community. The introduction of the police car placed a previously unknown strain on communication between the officer and citizen, but the automobile air conditioner catapulted police community relations backwards into the dark age.

The new, ambitious recruit will soon be converted by the field training officer or police department with a reactive philosophy. Every thinking, conscientious officer who's been employed long enough for his gun belt to stop squeaking and who has taken more than a dozen theft reports, knows that the only solution to the problem of crime is crime prevention. Reactive policing involves no crime prevention.

Reactive policing insures large amounts of future police work, an advantage not lost on the bureaucracy. Like medical doctors who refuse to practice preventive medicine, reactive officers can always justify their role. They need not fear not being needed. Reactive policing results in such inefficiency, it actually favors the criminal. It engages the officer in report taking when time spent on crime prevention would prove more productive. Reactive policing attempts to unring the bell.

Conversely, proactive policing involves maximizing observations of and interventions in the community. Proactive policing strives to maximize the quality and quantity of observations and interventions. Proactive policing does not mean aggressive law enforcement. The officer who frequently converses with many different people on his beat increases the number of interventions in the community, but not necessarily the number of enforcement actions. The officer who makes many vehicle stops, also maximizes the number of interventions, regardless of whether or not citations result.

By definition, proactive policing must involve every demographic group in the community. Proactive policing requires the officer to talk with the aged and with children, both sexes, all religions, representatives of every occupation, ethnic group, and race. The officer must discriminate in police discretion but must never discriminate in police community relations. This philosophy holds that for too long police have interacted only with suspects, criminals, victims, witnesses, and others related to traditional police situations. Obviously, in an applied sense, proactive policing must include reactive policing, but it includes more and goes far beyond reactive policing.

Considerable misunderstanding exists, even among police, about the nature and results of proactive policing. Some officers define it as arresting as many offenders as possible. Although an increased number of arrests is a predictible outcome of increased police curiosity, neither defines the other. Many individual officers in small town and rural policing exhibit very high rates of observations and interventions without corresponding high arrest rates. Separating arrest rates and proactive policing seems easy; separating proactive policing, police community relations, and reduced crime rates appears impossible.

Proactive policing results in effective policing, if reduced crime measures effective policing. One study showed a strong negative correlation between the number of moving vehicle citations and FI cards completed (a Field Interrogation card is a simple record the officer completes in the field about a person, including identifying information, location, and date and time. The subject is not arrested, cited or obligated in any way. FI cards are for police files only) and the number of armed robberies of all night service stations. This study surveyed many large cities throughout the United States. As more FI cards and "movers" were written, service station robberies decreased. As the number of FI cards and "movers" decreased, robberies increased. True, this might have been related to an intervening variable, such as the relative humidity, the ion effect, or whether or not the officer, or the robber for that matter, was bottle fed or breast fed as a baby. But again, conventional wisdom dictates that proactive policing reduces crime. This was a very direct, mechanical example. Proactive policing prevents much more crime in an indirect, often unseen, way.

The previous example included only offenders and police. With the community involved in proactive policing, crime drops by exponential factors. Proactive policing reduces the distance between the police and the policed. It helps insure and promote improved public safety. Proactive policing prevents unauthorized ringing of the bell.

Imagine a grid of two rows, three columns, and six cells. The three columns represent the three styles of policing, watchman, legalistic, and service. The two rows represent two philosophies of policing, reactive and proactive. Without much forcing, every individual police officer fits neatly into one of the six cells. Since most police departments are small town or rural, most police departments are properly classified in the proactive row, service column cell. Since an overwhelming majority of officers work for the relatively few big city police departments, and since these same police departments traditionally practice reactive policing, most officers, and consequently most policing, appear in the reactive row.

Community-based policing results from an elaboration of the proactive, service cell. Now imagine adding a third dimension to the grid. The first two axes are categorical, but the third axis is a continuum. It consists of a range of *police community relations* from extremely low and almost nonexistent, to extremely high and near perfect. There are still only six cells, but each of them now includes an infinite number of degrees. Community-based policing is not something that a community either has or doesn't have, but it is something that a community possesses in varying degrees. Like human behavior, community-based policing appears not black or white but different shades of gray.

The addition of this third dimension, and nothing else, permits measuring the effectiveness of a police department. If a community desires a reactive watchman policing, but the police department insists on policing in a legalistic style with a proactive philosophy, that police department would score low in effectiveness. They might write a lot of traffic citations and throw many a bloke in the slammer, but they police ineffectively. The police and the community sing from two different hymnals.

When a police department attempts to determine the needs and wants of the community in order to better provide services, that police department moves into its proper one of the six cells. When that police department makes a concerted effort to deliver those services it begins to move in a positive way along the third axis. It will become more effective as it improves and increases its interaction and communication with the people it serves.

Each small town or rural community usually presents one rather clear picture of its nature, spirit, or personality. This makes it considerably easier for the police department or chief to comprehend what the community wants and expects from the police. Larger towns are usually a mixture of several communities and appear very complex with a variety of personalities which never present one clear picture. A large city might be an almagamation of many different communities, or it might be a patchwork quilt. Either way, it will not present one accurate description that the police might use for direction in determining what the public expects from the police. One community in a big city might appear larger or more vocal or carry more political clout than the others; but the police, if they police effectively, must serve all the people and not just those of any one segment. Those who expect the police of a large city to satisfy most of the people most of the time sentence themselves to disappointment. The police of a large city deserve to claim some success if they manage to satisfy some of the people some of the time. Expecting the police of a large city to police the total city as effectively as small town and rural officers police is expecting the impossible. Comparing big city policing to small town and rural policing on a single scale of effectiveness or police community relations invites accusations of unfairness, as does measuring small town or rural policing with a single big city standard.

Such a comparison uses a standard of one to measure the other. Much of the negative stereotyping of small town and rural police results from evaluating them with big city standards. Judging big city policing by the quantity and quality of communication and interaction between the police department and the total community, in a sense, judges them with small town and rural standards. Few expect residents of larger cities to communicate and interact with the police; that would mean policing the community themselves, and the responsibility of policing belongs not to them but to the bureaucracy.

Big city policing can learn a lot, however, by studying small town and rural policing. The interpersonal communication and interaction between one small town or rural police officer and one person in the community is the foundation of community-based policing. This relationship seems timeless in policing. Long before the automobile air conditioner, even long before the automobile, this relationship between one officer and one citizen proved absolutely vital and critical to effective policing. Many things about policing changed, and continue to change, but the importance of that relationship will never change and cannot be overstated.

If quality and quantity interpersonal communication and interaction between the individual citizen and the individual police officer serve as the foundation of community-based policing, then the individual officer's attitude acts as the keystone to that foundation.

In its purest form, policing is talking and interacting with people. Although a few introverts manage to sneak into police work, police officers in general seem extroverted. Small town and rural officers appear comfortable with and usually enjoy talking and conversing with everyone. The small town or rural officer knows that every person, even children, represent at least one interesting tale. To the small town or rural officer, every person suggests a story. Social intercourse is not part of the job; it is the job. The wallflower or recluse can fit into many roles in the small town or rural community, but policing is not one of those. The hermit will not survive as a small town or rural police officer.

In the recruitment and hiring process of big city police departments, many forces act in concert to attract the introvert and repel the extrovert. The advertisement of job security, a retirement plan, and a higher starting salary all hint to the introvert of a job which promises high rewards in return for a minimum investment. Bureaucracies attract bureaucrats like bars attract drinkers. It is the very nature of the beast. Small town and rural police departments in contrast have poor or no retirement programs, fringe benefits, or high salaries to offer. In that sense, they attract the adventuresome, the outgoing, and the extroverted. The cynicism common to big city police departments can also cause even the extroverted officer to recoil into the secret, secure world of the bureaucracy and avoid the risk-taking involved in interacting with citizens.

The hiring process of bureaucratic police departments eliminates all except those who fit the cookie cutter mold of what they envision to be the ideal police officer. In reality, the process reflects the ideal employee of that particular bureaucracy. Should individualism, originality, or creativity somehow escape detection and slip into big city police work, it will be repressed and eliminated either during the officer's probationary period or forced into the cookie cutter of conformity. Frequently, the bureaucratic police department hires those who look, act, and think like the average officer on that police department, twenty years ago. If this continues, policing will never improve.

Hermits thrive on a big city police department. The introverted job applicant can anticipate a long tenure and an attractive retirement income when he is hired by the larger police department. If that person keeps his mouth shut, the radio turned on at all times, his brass and leather polished, and refrains from wrecking too many police cars, or jumping into bed with too many of the wrong people, he stands an above-average chance of also retiring as chief.

In the recruitment and hiring process of the small or rural police department, many forces act in concert to favor hiring the extroverted. The nonbureaucratic police department frequently attempts to hire those who are friendly, affable, and who will fit into the structure of existing police community relations. The emphasis concentrates on fitting into the community; fitting into the police department seems of secondary interest. On the big city police department, the individual must fit into the police department, or he does not fit in. On the small town or rural police department, the individual must fit into the community, or he will not be effective as a police officer. The big city police department is looking for the company-man-type person, and the small town or rural police department is looking for the people-type person. The big city police department hires those with an attitude identical to its own, but the small town or rural police department hires those with an attitude compatible with the most prevalent attitudes of the community.

The personable, small town or rural officer who enjoys socializing receives behavior reinforcement from both the community and the police department. Community members feel they have a voice, a friend, a contact in the police department, and they do. This represents a larger percentage of the community, when compared to big city residents who feel the same way. Not everyone who knows a small town or rural officer controls a voice in community affairs, but the feeling remains; and perhaps the perception is more important than reality.

Since the police and the community are so thoroughly interwoven in small towns and rural areas, many community members do have a say in police community relations and police affairs. Those same individuals would not be heard in larger cities. Input from citizens in police community relations more accurately reflects the community in small towns and rural areas. This input is extremely valuable, whether aired at a city council meeting or exchanged between one citizen and one officer. Input from community members which accurately represents the community and a receptive, caring police attitude constitute the major important ingredients of community-based policing. Both occur with a greater frequency in small towns and rural communities.

Community-based policing also provides somewhat of a surprising answer to the old issue, who will police the police. In small towns and rural areas the community polices the police, but not through any formal or even visible mechanism. In large cities the police are answerable to only the police, regardless of what the politicians say. Internal affairs controls the most deviant, and the police subculture controls all others.

Small town and rural police are answerable to the community. Gossip serves an important role here. Small town and rural citizens enjoy sharing information about each other, and especially about the police. The majority of small town residents know all about the dirty laundry of the police department, whereas the majority of big town residents own no knowledge of internal, or external, police problems. Only a few are interested in such.

The small town or rural chief often shares some control over the police with the citizens of the community. For an officer involved in a particularly sensitive or troublesome case, the community often judges whether the officer goes or stays. The officer on the small town or rural police department ultimately answers to the community. In an identical situation in a larger city, the community seldom or never provides input. The big city chief would not think of relinquishing one tiny bit of control. The chief, or his underlings, decides whether the officer stays or goes. The officer on the big city police department ultimately answers to the police department and no other person or group.

In larger cities, the police and their operations seem removed and segregated from the community. The police feel they know what is best for policing the community and themselves. In small towns and rural communities, the police and the citizens share common goals, values, and beliefs. Concensus dictates what is best for policing. They police themselves with community-based policing.

The scope of the perceived police role adds to community-based policing in small towns and rural jurisdictions, but subtracts from it in larger cities. The police role in small towns and rural communities seems broadly conceived. The small town or rural police officer is expected to be a jack of all trades and a master of most. The service orientation tends to remove all barriers as to what the police can and cannot do. Animal calls, for example, are common to all policing. People call the police when they need help and know of no one else to ask. The mad cat call at three o'clock on Sunday morning in the big city will result in a referral at the very most. In a small town that call will probably result in an officer being sent to help. Animal calls, checking on shut-ins, helping the elderly and handicaped, vacation homes, public assistance calls, suspicious persons, suspicious noises, suspicious circumstances, and millions of calls from people whose real but unspoken reason for calling the police is loneliness show only a few of the long list of calls that are much more likely to receive police attention and service on the small town or rural police department.

The fact that small town and rural police respond to such a wide range of calls and perform such a wide range of duties helps explain the advanced degree of police community relations enjoyed by small town and rural citizens and police alike. The attitudes of the officer and the citizen contribute to this. They both view a sweeping, all encompassing role as most appropriate. The refrain, this is not our job so we shouldn't be doing this, so commonly heard on big city police departments, seldom sounds in small town and rural policing. Healthy police community relations can only grow and flourish where the police serve and help the citizens in any way possible. When the citizen observes such a genuine attitude, he seems more likely to respect the police and respond in kind when provided an opportunity. In such a setting the police appear more likely to be viewed as neighbors than as impersonal law enforcement officers working for the city. It is only human nature to think better of those who have helped us, or stand nearby ready to help, than of those who never enter our world.

In larger cities the police role appears with greater frequency as limited and narrow. For example, in many big cities the police no longer respond to burglary reports. Mr. or Ms. Straight Arrow Citizen returns home after another hard day in a horrible job, only to find the front door open and many of his/her valuable possessions gone. This person suffers grievous injury. Burglary victims feel raped. Some criminal with no right to do so, trespassed and violated the victim. The victim also represses fears that he/she may never see their property again. So, as soon as they collect their wits, they do what all their instincts say do. They call the police because they are hurt, desperate, afraid. They want reassurance; and most importantly, they know the police will help them.

It is difficult, perhaps impossible, to imagine the pain and shock these victims resuffer when a faceless, mechanical voice informs them that because no suspects exist, the police will not respond and take a report. The victim wonders who develops suspects, apparently not the police. The victim is told to compile a list of missing property and bring it to the police department. What if the victim has no car? Does the police department only serve the affluent? If the police don't investigate burglaries, what do they do? The answer to this last question might entertain, were it not so sad. Big city police perform less traditional police work and more bureaucratic busy work each year. Big city departments exemplify self-fulfilling prophecies. Too busy in the past to do certain fundamental police tasks, like talk with the public and take theft reports, now they find themselves often too busy to do any police work. Bureaucratic efficiency reigns at an all time high, and overall police effectiveness sinks to an all time low.

This situation results in private police assuming more of the duties traditionally handled by public police. More private police officers exist than public police officers, and the total number of private police officers grows constantly. It represents a growth industry with no major limitations in the foreseeable future. Located primarily in the larger metropolitan areas, they somehow manage to find the time to provide personalized service to their customers, who are all paying customers. They provide no services to the poor.

Perhaps a large police department in the West illustrates the most absurd example. They do not take stolen automobile reports in the field or on the phone. If a person leaves home one morning enroute to work only to discover the trusty, rusty steed stolen, then it will do no good to call the police for help. They will not respond. They will not send an officer to take a report, they will not take the report by telephone, and they will not look for the car until after the victim files a report. To file this report the victim must walk, hitchhike, or beg a ride to the police department. They will not give the victim a ride to the police department. "Be honest with me, lady, does this car really look like a yellow cab?" Obviously, such a policy discriminates unfairly against the poor or anyone without two cars. The opportunity costs of big city police retreating from traditional police tasks cause erosion of police community relations, an almost total void of community-based policing, and an unprecedented low police effectiveness.

Such examples remain virtually unknown in small town and rural policing. Blatant disregard for the victim might cause at least one officer, and perhaps more, to be fired. Such obnoxious, impersonal, ignoring of the victim's expectation of police help remains unthinkable and inexcusable. The written rule on the large police department means a prohibited exception on the small police department. Small town and rural police actually capitalize on these situations. These cases provide the police an opportunity to perform, to shine, to impress the victim as they help the victim, to win a convert for the police cause, to spring into action. Like the firefighter when the fire bell alarms, small town and rural police see a citizen's call for help as the time to do their duty. Small town and rural police welcome the duty and responsibility of police responding with sincere personal service to that burglary victim, auto theft victim, or any other person who believes they need police help. People insure that small town and rural police departments deliver human help, while bureaucracies require that large police departments only react in a bureaucratic manner.

Such examples of police service do not go unrewarded in small towns and rural communities. Like in big cities, policing here becomes a self-fulfilling prophecy. Success is expected and it is achieved. A high quality of police community relations rewards the investment of a high quantity of police community relations. People expect police to respond in a sincere, caring, efficient manner; and their expectations are fulfilled. Police expect the public to communicate and join in this joint adventure called policing, and again these expectations do not go unfulfilled in small towns and rural communities.

Viewed from the perspective of the small town philosophy, effective policing seems a circular chain. Certain attitudes of citizens and police contribute to improved police community relations, which in turn promotes community-based policing. As community-based policing advances, it inevitability leads to significant increases in police effectiveness. As police effectiveness increases so does public safety, the quality of life, and even the mental health of the overall community. As all of these things happen, the attitudes of citizens and police become more positive and less negative. It is only human nature to feel at least some pride in our own accomplishments. When people police themselves via community-based policing, the only effective way to police, they rightfully feel proud of their accomplishment. They did it. They did it all by themselves. They did not rely on the city, the bureaucracy, a large remote police department, any group of authorities or experts, or any other group of strangers to come in and police them. They found success by policing themselves and they know it. Nothing succeeds like success.

The Police Foundation, after its creation in 1971, became the foremost private research organization to study policing. Its contributions to improving policing appear both large and significant. It underwrites numerous studies and research projects. Skolnick and Bayley completed one such study, an attempt to develop evidence indicating what police might do that would result in "perceptible increases" in public safety and police effectiveness. (Big city policing remains so ineffective that significant or notable improvement is no longer expected, the public will be happy with only a perceptible improvement.) They spent two years observing six big city police departments. Their findings reveal powerful suggestions for improving policing in large cities. Their findings also, without exception, reverberate testimony to the strengths of small town and rural policing, community-based policing, and improved police community communication and interaction.

Like many police scientists and writers, Skolnick and Bayley err in not constructing sufficient safeguards to prevent the reader from generalizing. They wrote of American police, police officers, and American cities, as though those six police departments represented all U.S. police.

Their research and findings are rife with irony for anyone who appreciates small town and rural police. Their findings make only a partial list of the attributes of small town and rural policing, and the researchers carefully avoid giving any credit to those who seem the most knowledgeable in this subject, practice community-based policing daily, and respect and cherish the concept. Their book makes no mention of August Vollmer, the first police chief to require that his officers study, understand, and practice community-based policing.

It is a little known fact that the Police Foundation discriminates against small town and rural police. The Police Foundation does not award grants to populations of fewer than 100,000 or to police departments having less than 100 officers. Apparently, they feel above researching the smaller police departments, obviously believing nothing could be learned; but they are not above stealing a valuable concept which has always been free to serious students, and claiming it for the sovereignty of big city policing in the name of the Police Foundation. One final irony exists in the title of Skolnick and Bayley's book, *The New Blue Line*. Wise police officers have always known the only policing that consistently works is self policing. The officer who walked the same beat for thirty-eight years in Chicago, the functionally illiterate sheriff in rural Mississippi — all thinking police officers understand that people either police themselves or they are not policed. Wearing a new blue coat, the old blue line reemerges.

Old wine in new bottles remains good wine, regardless of who stomped the grapes. A profound truth remains just as true and just as valuable, regardless of who repeats it. Skolnick and Bayley did a superb job of delivering the message to big city police departments. There exists little doubt their book will, in time, contribute greatly to improving policing in many large cities. The vast majority of all police officers gladly and quickly transcend any petty claims of ownership or originality in the interest of improving any part of policing.

To say that the police cannot police by themselves makes an understatement to small town and rural police. They know partial community involvement results only in partial police effectiveness. Even this remains more desirable than no police effectiveness. Small town and rural police know that total community involvement seldom results in anything but total police effectiveness. Community involvement and police effectiveness directly correlate. An increase in one almost always accompanies an increase in the other.

In community-based policing, form usually follows function, but function seldom follows form. If big city police departments are to learn and profit from small town and rural policing, they must incorporate the underlying attitudes, philosophies, and fundamentals of community-based policing. Constructing a program identical in form to a plan of community-based policing does not guarantee success. The function of community-based policing, the attitudes, spirit, and the philosophy must also exist for a program to succeed. If the latter exist, there is little chance the program will fail, regardless of the form. People from the community and patrol officers working together make the function and power of community-based policing. Those people from the community must be an accurate sample of the total community population. If they fairly represent the total community and if both patrol and management sincerely want improved policing, then little exists to prevent success.

Big city police department administrators have long held that they need more officers to wage war on crime. This is a predictable position of any bureaucracy. But increasing the number of police officers on a police department never produces a corresponding reduction in crime. Nor does it produce increased public satisfaction, increased police effectiveness, or any other indicator of improvement in policing. The lesson here from small town and rural police teaches that more police are not needed as frequently as are better police. To increase quantity with no concern for quality is so unreasonable that only the most unsophisticated, or a bureaucracy, would attempt such.

Whether one, two, or no officers arrive to handle a burglary report matters little if none of the officers have a sincere, helping, humanistic attitude. Virtually all victims want and need a sympathetic person, not a report taker, to help them through their ordeal. Small town and rural police must be generalists, able to handle every kind of police situation. They therefore become more sensitive to human needs, behavior, and motivations. They actually become better qualified to satisfy the citizen. They know how to please the customer, and they realize the value of a satisfied customer. Community-based policing cannot happen until each officer sincerely adopts such an attitude and develops these skills. The best community-based policing efforts will be quickly sabotaged by one officer with a bad attitude.

Big city police administrators bemoan the tragic shortage of money. They argue that the police do not produce more results because of grossly unfair under-budgeting. This, too, becomes a self-fulfilling prophecy of sorts. The next year at budget hearings, the chief can say, "I told you so, we just did not have enough money." The best of bureaucratic arguments seems the most ridiculous. Throwing more money on the fire will never extinguish it.

Small town and rural policing presents convincing evidence that effective policing does not require tons of money. The lesson for big city policing appears similiar to the last one. How much money a police department acquires is not nearly as important as how the police department spends money. The police dollar spent on an investment of police community relations will always produce the highest return. Since this involves a long-term investment with no dividends immediately visible, difficulties arise. Putting the money into fighting drugs will show immediate results in the form of front pages picturing mountains of dope and weapons. Administrators of large police departments love this because they now claim proof positive to show the taxpayers that their tax dollars are being spent wisely, even though guns and dope cannot be indicted, tried, convicted, or imprisoned. On large police departments many appearances of efficiency exist without hints of effectiveness.

Small town and rural police offer persuasive evidence that the range of possible inexpensive or cost-free community-based policing programs seem limited only by the imagination. These programs range from the short and simple to the long and complex. They include programs best identified as police community relations, police juvenile relations, educational, entertainment, socializers, athletic, and public awareness, among many others. All these programs possess only one common requirement. They all require police officers with sincerity, desire, and some initiative. They do not all require money.

Perhaps the greatest myth about policing ever fostered on the public involves the debate about the effect of police patrol on crime rates. The battle lines are clearly drawn with some claiming police patrol presence, or police visibility, deters crime, while others with an equally strong argument counter that police patrol has absolutely no effect on crime. One of the largest and most polished controlled experiments ever undertaken in police science addressed this question. The Kansas City study, as it came to be known, concluded that motorized police patrol does not significantly affect crime. Critics of this study were, and still are, loud and many. Big city police department administrators want nothing to do with anything that challenges tradition or holds the potential to decrease personnel. Generally, all police management, with most of the exceptions found in small town and rural police departments, believes that police patrol deters crime. This premise forms a cornerstone of policing. Routine patrol is a police phrase used by all officers throughout recent history.

Whether or not patrol deters crime clouds and hides the real issue. The debate only serves to obfuscate and even bury the real issue. The Kansas City Preventive Patrol Experiment was valid, reliable, and correct in its conclusion that vehicular patrol *alone* does not deter crime. If it did, drivers could be hired much cheaper than officers; and they could drive around for eight hours detering crime. The Kansas City study did result in a few scholars reasoning one step beyond to the real issue: a realization that the number of police cars on the street, or even the number of officers, does not correlate with crime; but what those officers do can greatly influence the crime rate.

The Kansas City study assumed that all police officers do the same thing while on patrol, nothing. Although that assumption may be made with safety about certain police departments, it does not hold true for many other police departments. Although, as already explained, most officers practice reactive policing, most police departments subscribe to a police philosophy more accurately described as proactive.

Proactive policing deters crime, irrespective of the method of patrol, the number of cars or officers, or the size of the police department. Proactive policing deters crime because it involves people interacting with people, police interacting with citizens. Motorized patrol does not deter crime because automobiles and empty key hooks on the motor pool board cannot perform any police function. The bureaucracy often gives the appearance that policing means cars, breath testing equipment, night sticks with metal tips, soft body armor, sap gloves, and expensive communications and computer hardware; but all of these are nothing but tools to make the officer's job easier and safer. Only people, never a bureaucracy, can police. A bureaucracy cannot police or deter crime.

Unfortunately, some big city police department administrators miss the ultimate meaning of the Kansas City study. It should not be interpreted as meaning the patrol officer is not always necessary but as meaning we need to rethink what we want the police to do. What do the thousands of good, hardworking, law abiding citizens, the ones who pay for police services, think of police effectiveness? It is possible they were generally satisfied in Kansas City. Perhaps Kansas Citians felt comfortable tolerating their crime rate. That variable must be considered when we attempt to measure police effectiveness. It just might be that Kansas City was receiving exactly the kind of policing it wanted, at the time of the study.

Even if the Kansas City community was not happy with its police, the implications of the study seem encouraging. By training, educating, and supervising our police differently, we change the way they police. The small town and rural police experience shows that all policing does not mean the same thing. The process affects the output. If a community is satisfied with its crime rate and its police department, then do not disturb the process or the output. Cities that sincerely want to reduce crime and violence will profit most by studying programs and concepts of proactive and community-based policing. They must realize that their police can be more than reactive, and they can change their police. If citizens do not do it, it will not be done. Any community, large or small, that waits for their police to initiate change, wastes valuable time.

Another old, heated debate in police circles concerns the pros and cons of one-officer cars versus two-officer cars. Generally, the battle line separates the officers who work the street, and advocate two officers to a car, from the administration, who keep an eye on expenditures and insist that one officer to a car is in no way more dangerous. Resolution of this issue was reached in a most objective manner. Insurance claims records indicate that one-officer units appear no more, or less, dangerous than two-officer units. Small town and rural police generally speaking would not know what to do with two to a vehicle.

In many big cities the wisdom gained only from working the street many years prevails over social research. Officers are deployed two per car in those areas where they perceive conditions jeopardizing the safety of a single officer. A few small town and rural police departments assign two officers per car when hazardous conditions exist and they can afford it. Otherwise, alternative methods must be considered. Many small town and rural police departments discourage their officers from going into a dangerous situation alone. Others outright prohibit it. The prohibition makes it easier for the conscientious officer to remain safe. Some officers, found on every size police department, thrive on danger, the more the better. These adrenalin junkies fill a necessary role in policing.

Officers relatively overconcerned with personal safety are not un-common and are not found predominately on any one size police depart-ment. They are also important to policing. They serve as a sober reminder of that most primary of all police priorities, survival. The ma-jority of officers, those in the middle of the bell curve, possess sufficient courage and a healthy respect for danger. Police officers probably average somewhat higher on a risk-taking scale than does a cross section of the public. Police courage does not seem to vary by size of police de-partment. Police officers appear to be action-oriented risk-takers. More research will help determine if insurance claims files might reveal a cor-relation between injuries and police department size.

Patrol is the heart and life's blood of policing. All policing is done by the patrol officer in the field. Everything else in policing exists to sup-port the patrol officer. The importance of the street patrol officer seems frequently downplayed, but no one can overstate the importance of this key pivotal position. This aids in understanding why so many of the ma-jor controversial issues in policing relate to patrol. All other issues ap-pear incidental.

A common assumption in policing for decades held that saturation patrol reduced crime. Obviously related to the previously discussed concept of patrol deterring crime, many believed saturation patrol of-fered the ultimate deterrent. No criminal would be so stupid as to try to commit a crime with a patrol car on every block. Some larger police departments rely heavily on saturation patrol in troublesome areas. Both of these concepts evolved from the premise that the mere pres-ence of police acts as a deterrent to crime. Many still believe that the presence of many police units prevents crime, and the more police cars present, the more crime will be prevented. One seems to logically follow the other.

The same explanation destroys both the preventive patrol theory and the saturation patrol theory. The Kansas City study debunked two po-lice myths. The number of police cars, or police motorcycles, or officers in any given area makes little difference. What those officers do makes the difference. Counting the number of police units and expecting that figure to relate to crime assumes that all police officers do the same thing. Every day hundreds of thousands of officers violate this assump-tion. Policing is what the officers do, not how many officers there are. English teachers and wordsmiths cringe, but policing is always an active verb; it is never a passive verb or a noun or a gerund. Policing is action. Policing is doing; it is what many police officers do.

The wisdom of twenty-twenty hindsight now makes it clear that saturation patrol, like preventive patrol, hides the real issue. The real issue remains what the police in the field do, or don't do.

Saturation patrol may give a misleading appearance. Displacing some crime to adjacent areas, it causes the appearance of crime reduction. Even this observation makes the dangerous assumption that the volume of crime remains constant in the control area. Drug trafficking in South Florida provides a clear example on a larger scale. Intense, concentrated law enforcement efforts fighting the drug smugglers in the 1980s in Florida caused dope runners to move their activities to other states, according to the more optimistic. This is the displacement theory. It assumes crime remains relatively constant. Many alert thinking police from Key Largo to San Diego express fear that none of the dopers move because of displacement; they simply multiply in numbers and present the appearance of being displaced. Sure, a few individual cases indicate a burned transporter confesses to changing his routes and M.O. because of police pressure; but he cannot speak for the smugglers who moved in and took his former place.

Crime displacement theory offers the most obvious and logical armchair explanation for those bent on proving that saturation patrol does not work. In a curious bit of twisted irony, scholarly investigation, when focusing on the police, only wants to count heads and strongly resists any suggestion of examining activity; but when the focus turns to criminals, the tendency changes to scrutinize what they do and avoid all head counting attempts. Traditionally, those studying patrol sought any correlation between police headcount and criminal activity. Police thinkers contend a more important and meaningful relationship exists between police activity and criminal headcount.

Another confused police science topic involves the frequency with which serious crime is encountered. Again, the explanation involves generalization. A police department is observed, a conclusion reached, and then that conclusion is generalized to include all policing. If a reactive police operation is monitored, the study will conclude police seldom encounter serious or violent crime. Conversely, if proactive police are watched, one will conclude that police frequently interrupt or cross violent or serious crime. If the inquirer asks an individual officer, the response depends on that officer's own orientation. Such stark contrast is innate to policing.

The chemistry of the policed also contributes to the variance in this issue. Police in an upper-class bedroom community may encounter a minimum of violence and felony crime. While in a nearby town, notorious for knuckles and buckles, the police operate shuttle busses to the jail. However, proactive officers argue that human nature does not vary so much as to allow for a crime-free community. They contend that even the quietest, most Norman Rockwellian community imaginable contains some crime. Finding it presents a challenge to the proactive officer. Perhaps those who argue that police seldom encounter serious crime never rode with a proactive officer. Like J. Edgar Hoover, they spend much time in the office studying statistics and little time in the street studying people and crime. They give the impression they never originated a felony in progress, never caught a burglar, never saw a DWI stop explode into a felony, or never experienced a minor traffic violation suddenly turn into a major dope case complete with closure and newly found informants. Because it results from attitude, the frequency that police encounter serious crime is more a function of police activity than of any other independent variable.

The effect of response time, if any, on the probability of crime solving provides yet another unresolved issue of police patrol. Some feel the sooner police arrive after a crime occurs, the more likely that the crime will ultimately be solved. Others present the results of studies indicating no correlation between the two variables. The total evidence appears equally divided. A possibility exists that any relationship depends on the type of offense, or call, and the time frame involved. It seems undeniable that seconds can save a life and minutes can interrupt and identify a felon. Conversely, no one argues that hours save lives or catch felons in the act. The data addressing the issue is less than complete and not above criticism.

While living in a tiny, efficiency apartment in West Oakland, California, my wife and I returned home one day to interrupt a burglary in progress. As I unlocked and tried to open the front door, it jerked tight against the night chain, alerting the burglar who bolted like superman and flew through a small rear window. We telephoned police from a friend's apartment; and they arrived in minutes via black and whites, unmarked units, motorcycles, and a helicopter. Within an hour the suspect was arrested. Years later, while living in Nacogdoches, Texas, I suffered a seizure and entered a coma. In our car my wife followed the ambulance which followed a police car driven by one of my former students. She said speeds exceeded 100 miles per hour. The doctor said it was a close call and minutes saved my life. I moved to an even smaller Texas town a few months after leaving the hospital and never saw that officer after my wife's high speed chase. Ironically, he possibly never knew he saved my life.

Police enemies, disguised as students and researchers of the police, and others, who for reasons unknown to all, want to rob the police of the credit and recognition they deserve. They insist that crimes are solved by luck, divine intervention, astute citizens, and many other means, none of which relate in any form to police efforts. The Rand Corporation did a study to determine who solves crime. This think tank, unlike the Police Foundation, harbors no obvious prejudices against small town and rural police. The Rand study surprised detectives, criminal investigators, and more than a few patrol officers. It found that of all solved crime, the officer on the street solves fully 90 percent. Another 9 percent could have been solved by the officer in the field, and only 1 percent of all solved crime requires the expertise of a detective or criminal investigator.

One possible explanation for these findings begs for attention. The officer in the field deciphers most solved crime because he works closer to the people, the crime, and the community. He knows the crime scene and constantly mingles with people in and around the crime scene long before and long after the crime. The officer promoted (demoted?) to detective leaves the street and thereby loses contact with the people in the community and informants. The link between a patrol officer and the citizen constitutes the only link between the police department and the community and the only correlation between police patrol and police effectiveness.

What the police do and how they do it determine the product or results of police patrol. Size of agency, number of police cars on the street, chemistry of the community, ratio of police cars to citizens, number of officers to a car, amount of money budgeted, ratio of officers to citizens, response time, and several other variables contribute little or nothing to police effectiveness. The attitude and philosophy of the officer on the street, the man in the arena, determine what the police do on patrol and the results of that activity. The patrol officer on the street will always remain the life and soul of policing. Policing results from nothing other than the efforts of the individual patrol officer. Police effectiveness can be no greater than, or no less than, the performance of the police officer on the street.

Continuing the examination of effectiveness, The Police Foundation sponsored study of six large police departments found four essential elements of innovation necessary for police improvement: *police-community reciprocity, decentralization of command, reorientation of patrol* (foot patrol), and *civilianization.*

First, police community reciprocity preceeds all police effectiveness. Big city police departments, determined in their lonely masochistic struggle, prove this truism daily. Community police reciprocity and small town and rural police overlap as almost synonymous concepts. The small town philosophy discussed earlier depends on reciprocity between the community and individuals, or groups of individuals, for survival. Without reciprocity the small town or rural community ceases to exist as an attitude. Small town philosophy considers the police department a vital and integral part of the whole, not an overgrown, costly, necessary evil, best left to the worry of others. In small towns and rural areas the individual retains a feeling of considerable responsibility for community governance, including policing. By comparison, the individual in big cities relinquishes feelings of responsibility for governance and policing to specialized groups, who boast of their expertise and skill. As responsibility transfers from the individual to a larger group, no one must any longer bear responsibility. Reciprocity exists only between individual human beings. A bureaucracy cannot reciprocate with personal human feelings and responses. Bureaucracies reciprocate only with bureaucratic methods and responses. When a bureaucracy claims responsibility for policing, no one, certainly not the individual officer on the street, is responsible for doing police work.

The citizen requesting that a particular officer handle his/her case asks for nothing more than personal attention. Calls of this type occur in all size police departments, but small town and rural police departments receive a higher relative percentage of them. The individual citizen, a part of the community, contributes to police community reciprocity by requesting personal attention. The police department, also a part of the community, reciprocates by honoring the request, or carefully explaining why the request cannot be met and the available alternatives. Only if convenience permits will the larger police department honor such a request. In small towns and rural communities informality prevails between citizens and officers and among officers, regardless of rank. Here the police department responds, or reciprocates, to the citizen's call for help by sending a human with a first as well as a last name and perhaps, no badge number what-so-ever. A high probability exists that the officer knows the caller or at least knows someone the caller knows.

In larger police departments strict rules of formality permeate thought and action. Here the police department responds to citizens' calls for help with military bearing. All the officers look and behave alike. Numbered, like prisoners, they delight in giving it to citizens as identification. Bureaucratic anonymity replaces human individualism. Their nametags, or lack thereof, show that none of the officers possess first names, only initials; while others claim no name at all, only a number. Communication between officers is more formal than in smaller police departments. Titles of rank must be used and respected. "Since we are such good friends call me by my first name. It is Sergeant." Officers on larger police departments believe that they must remain aloof and business like to insure respect from the citizenry. Showing a personal side displays a weakness in the world of the bureaucracy.

Next, The Police Foundation sponsored study emphasized the importance of decentralization of command as a means of repairing the bridge between the police and the community. Decentralization of command works in several ways to narrow the gap between the police department and the community. Physically it decreases the distance between the two. The less affluent frequently profit the most from decentralization efforts. Anytime the police make themselves more accessible to a broader range of people in the community, they automatically improve police community relations. The police must carefully guard against losing sight of the philosophy and goal in the mechanics of a decentralization program. The small, storefront neighborhood substation looks great on the drawing board but will fail miserably if the location does not take advantage of the daily movement of people in the neighborhood or if the officers assign to work it possess less than a sincere and positive attitude.

Decentralization of command never presents great difficulties for small town and rural police departments because of their size. They model for others to copy. Large police departments, interested in community-based policing via decentralization of command, will profit more from closely examining and studying small town police operations than from trying to emulate programs of other large police departments. Larger police departments must seek the function; the form will work itself out. Function follows form only by coincidence.

Small town and rural police work in a test tube. Leaders on large police departments who want to study one particular concept, such as decentralization of command, will often find it isolated and clearly defined on smaller police departments. Small town and rural police departments form a valuable but ignored police science laboratory. They provide the opportunity to study policing in its simplest, purest form. Scientists wanting to study a phenomenon begin with the smallest unit that contains the same characteristics as the larger structure. Small town and rural police represent the protozoans of the police world. Scientific inquiry of policing properly begins with the least contaminated sample. Perhaps as a sample, small town and rural policing contains more hallmark traits and fewer extraneous features of policing than do other size police departments. If a study seeks to examine a variable of the majority of police officers, that study should focus on the officers employed by the larger police departments. Researchers investigating a variable of the majority of police chiefs, or police departments, cannot avoid focusing on small town and rural chiefs, or police departments, to maintain academic intregrity. Perhaps more can be learned about the nature of policing itself and police community relations by studying small town and rural policing than by researching the policing of large cities. Small town and rural police present a microcosmic study of policing. They represent the epitome of policing.

The Police Foundation study also listed reorientation of patrol as a required element of innovation for more effective policing of big cities. Fundamental concepts of patrol reorientation include steps to improve attitudes of street officers toward the public and physical programs intended to make the police more accessible to the public.

Few patrol reorientation programs contain more promise than *foot patrol*. Viewed negatively, foot patrol forces the officer into the community. He can no longer atrophy in a police car. Foot patrol cannot force the person to practice good police community relations, nothing can do that; but it does force the officer to take that dreaded first step towards good police community relations, getting out of the car. Viewed in a positive light, foot patrol gives the officer an opportunity to meet and talk with people, develop informants, identify potential police concerns, observe the community, learn about human behavior, laugh, and enjoy police work. Foot patrol, in short, gives the officer the occasion to police.

A vague but necessary distinction exists between foot patrol and walking patrol. Foot patrol involves an attitude which attempts to maximize face-to-face encounters with citizens, average community members who do not routinely interact with the police. Walking patrol means the physical method of an officer walking and patrolling a geographical beat. Officers assigned to patrol in vehicles may adopt a foot patrol attitude; but only those assigned to walk a beat, eight hours a day, five days a week, use walking patrol.

The Vollmer philosophy never changes. The officer must get out of the car to police. Taxi cab and bus drivers, as well as race car and truck drivers improve their skills and perform their occupational tasks with a steering wheel. Police officers do not. The car serves the officer as a splendid tool but nothing more. Countless attempts to substitute a car for police work inevitably fail. For decades some police tried to explain ineffectiveness with perceived limitations placed on them by certain case law. Using their own vernacular, they spoke figuratively of being handcuffed. Ironically, the police themselves, not the courts, impose the greatest restriction on policing. They handcuffed themselves when emphasis was shifted from foot patrol to vehicular patrol. The strength of the concept of foot patrol lies with the thorough intergration of the police and the community. Likewise, the weakness of the concept of vehicular patrol concerns the distance and inaccessibility of the police.

The arguments for vehicular patrol and against foot patrol seem endless. They include many advantages and disadvantages but seldom make any mention of police community relations, the essence of effective policing, or human laziness. Effective policing cannot coexist with police laziness. Police work presents officers with a free choice, leave the car and work or sit in the car and relax. Police administrators cultivate an atmosphere that rewards the latter and discourages the former.

Foot patrol involves an attitude, rather than a fixed method. The officer assigned to a predominately residential neighborhood can see the futility of a walking patrol in certain areas. In contrast, that same officer can never ignore a chance to exit the vehicle and talk with the idle citizen and achieve police effectiveness. A retired gentleman I knew lived directly across the street from a parking lot and gas pump used by municipal police and sheriff's deputies. He spent the last years of his life sitting on his front porch watching the world go by. One exit from the lot channelled vehicles so that less than forty feet separated drivers from this man. Aware that I possessed some knowledge of police and their operations, he asked why police officers appeared so grim, never smiling, returning his wave, or even acknowledging his existence. His own totally unscientific survey found not a single officer who would return his greeting. Sad.

Many patrol areas, or beats, do not include settings that lend themselves to the nineteenth century walking foot patrol. However, only in those patrol areas without crime or people can the officer expect to police effectively from inside the car. Officers who believe in and practice the foot patrol attitude but who are not assigned a beat where they can pound the bricks enter and exit their vehicle many times, even dozens of times, during one eight hour shift. For those officers, the vehicle may increase the effectiveness of walking patrol by permitting more visits with more people scattered throughout the assigned beat.

Officers assigned an area with a potential walking beat enjoy the best that policing offers. Positioned ideally to communicate and interact with people, this officer learns a myriad of intricate details necessary for superb policing. The officer's close proximity to the public implants a feeling in the citizen of nearness to the police plus a sense of security and safety.

This proximity enables the officer to monitor the pulse and assess the policing desires of the community. Police cannot deliver effective services until they know rather specifically what the community or neighborhood expects. The officer who practices the foot patrol attitude remains closely tuned to the temperament, personality, and expectations of the community. The police department, regardless of size, with enough of these officers polices with firm confidence; but the police department with few or none of these officers polices with a shaky uncertainty. The officer sporting a shiny pants seat who polices through a windshield frowns and wonders what the savages and scrots plan and conspire. The officer determined to overcome the suffocating chokehold of an automobile smiles with the knowledge and contentment of one in step with his total environment.

For those willing to study, other methods of patrol contain clues explaining the advantages of foot patrol and disadvantages of police patrolling in cars. When asked, police invariably list the leading advantage of mounted patrol, an officer on horseback, as the improved observation position. Then they reel off numerous other perceived advantages such as psychological factors, crowd control, maneuverability, and versatility. They miss, or ignore, the most important. Like music, horses possess a universal appeal to people. Virtually everyone likes horses. Young and old alike approach the mounted officer, not to talk police, but to talk horse. The horse melts the icy curtain between police and public. Anybody who rides a horse can't be all bad. Large, heavyweight motorcycles invoke opposite public reactions. Used by police for many of the same reasons as horses, behemoth motorcycles, complete with high-top black-booted, helmeted riders, probably intimidate the public more than any other police activity. The visitor to Washington, D. C., intrigued like me by policing, cannot fail to note the police use of motor scooters, motor bikes, and even lightweight motorcycles. The public image of police motorcycles parallels the image the public holds of motorcyclists in general. Apparently, the Washington, D. C. police department does not resent looking and acting like the community. The public finds it easier approaching an officer on horseback or on a motor scooter, than one in a car.

Police cars project an intimidating image to many. Citizens hesitate to approach the force and power of the state for anything but business. In sharp contrast, the lone officer presents a human picture. People try not to see the police car but find ignoring an officer standing nearby impossible. Body language makes talking to an officer in a car awkward at best, but the officer skilled in nonverbal communications controls the tone of face-to-face encounters without the car door barrier. With the officer outside the police vehicle, the citizen feels more equal, less overwhelmed. Foot patrol transfers the onus of initiating conversation from the individual citizen to the individual police officer. Reduced to its simplest terms, police community relations becomes the responsibility of the police, not the community.

Studies indicate walking patrols do not significantly deter crime. However, some of those same studies show a majority of the public, especially downtown business owners, express a strong preference for walking police patrols. Some business owners say they like walking patrols, even if they do little to prevent crime. Once again, perception appears more important than reality. Perceptive listeners believe these citizens tell the police world they enjoy talking and interacting with police. Perhaps the community desires the opportunity to like its police. Many residents of larger cities experience high crime rates and low police contact rates. Even if higher police contact rates do not influence crime rates, more face-to-face interaction between individuals and their police results in citizens feeling an increased satisfaction with their police. That translates into improved police effectiveness. Walking patrols and the foot patrol philosophy produce effective policing.

The foot patrol philosophy and walking beats both occur with a greater frequency in the world of small town and rural policing. The lone wolf law enforcement officer who wears his patrol car like a gunbelt occurs with a damaging frequency on larger police departments but appears only as an anomaly on smaller police departments. Small town and rural residents expect and receive personal service from the police. This includes officers who are friendly and personable at all times, not merely when a complaint or crime occurs. These citizens pay their police to protect and serve, not ride around in a police car. Small town and rural community residents knew long before the Kansas City study that automobiles do not make police officers.

Finally, the Police Foundation study discussed civilianization as a prerequisite to improving the policing of big cities. Civilianization involves employing civilians to perform tasks traditionally handled by police officers. Positions such as dispatchers, file clerks, property room personnel, photographers, and even crime scene technicians do not require police skills. In some situations civilian employees bring greater expertise to a particular role than do the police. Civilians do not command the higher salaries and fringe benefits, thus saving the city considerable money. However, integration of the police and the community resulting from civilianization looms as the chief benefit.

After civilianization the community feels like they supply more input into police operations. The appearance of secrecy that cloaks a big city police department begins to vanish with civilianization. The bridge between the police and the community now sees civilian as well as police travelers. The police are not entirely immune to the benefits. Civilianization causes the police to seriously reconsider long-held beliefs and attitudes that gave birth to the "us versus them" mind set. Suddenly, some of *them* work for the same employer as some of *us* and even suffer the same boss and problems.

Civilianization may occur in the police station, in the field, or both. Civilianization can free the officer in the field from such duties as vehicle accident investigation, abandoned auto calls, crime scene processing, and countless public service calls which mean so little to the police and so much to the caller.

The concept of community service officer evolved on a few large city police departments to address the need for improved delivery of police services. The job title gives cause for cynical amusement. Police departments establishing separate community service officer positions apparently do not require their police officers to do community service work. In small town and rural policing the role of police officer remains inseparable from the role of community service officer. The two exist as indistinguishable. In large cities with private police shouldering more traditional police duties, civilians assuming police duties in the station house, and community service officers policing in the field, the need for armed, uniformed, vehicular patrol shrivels. Perhaps motorized patrol as it is now known in large cities will regress and merge with SWAT teams (Special Weapons And Tactics) then disappear entirely.

Small town and rural police rely heavily on civilianization for survival. If they depended totally on police resources, as so many larger police departments try to do, the police effort would prove insignificant, ineffective, and often unnoticeable. Without bureaucratic support and backing, small town and rural police must trust in the community and civilianization for continuation. What the big town police department takes for granted, the small town police department must never ignore.

Many small town and rural police departments employ civilians as dispatchers but require the employee to also perform many other duties. Job descriptions, when they exist, for civilians in small town and rural police departments usually do not cover the wide range of tasks performed by the individual. Their roles remain crowded and clouded with detail. In contrast, civilians working for big city police departments can expect a clearly defined, written outline of their roles. Bureaucratization requires a precise delineation of roles.

Small town and rural police suffer the disadvantages of the absence of a bureaucracy. They must compensate and overcome. They hire civilians, recruit volunteers, and construct reserve programs to help better serve the community. When small town and rural police need help, they turn to the community, not inward to the police department, the bureaucracy, or the budget.

Civilianization, reorientation of patrol, and decentralization of command represent efforts directed toward increasing police community reciprocity. A higher degree of police community reciprocity characterizes small town and rural police and distinguishes them from all other police. Small town and rural police historically rely on civilians, both paid and unpaid, in the station house and field, as a fully integrated crucial part to complement the delivery of police services. Community service officers, cleverly disguised as police officers, perform all the police services, and more, required by the small town or rural community.

Small town and rural police view decentralization of command like fish view water. Their experience reassures them that no other world exists, and they cannot survive without it. Big town police departments survive only within the bureaucracy; small town police departments survive only without the bureaucracy. The Police Foundation study acknowledges by innuendo the contribution small town and rural police make to police innovation by existing as the epitome of command decentralization.

Small town and rural police never lost their orientation to patrol. Therefore, they possess no need for a reorientation of patrol. People in small towns and rural communities generally express satisfaction with the services delivered by the police. This translates to a satisfaction with the orientation of police patrol. Conservative by nature, small town and rural people see no reason to change, or reorient, the police. When problems do arise with the police, citizens view them as problems created by humans, not by organizational charts or orientation. Tar and feather the rascals and maybe chase them out of town, but don't reorient the police department. Dissatisfied citizens in the big city blame the system, the bureaucracy. They attack the process, patrol, giving rise to a reorientation of patrol. Dissatisfied citizens in small towns and rural areas blame the system, the police department, and attack the process, the individual officer involved. The bureaucracy shields the individual from personal attacks of incompetency and inefficiency.

The give and take, interdependence, and mutual sharing aspects of police community reciprocity continue to characterize small town and rural police and differentiate them from other police. Studying police community reciprocity conjures *deja vu.* Police community reciprocity rings hauntingly similar to police community relations. But a good book, with a new cover, remains forever a good book. Effective police community relations and effective policing remain inseparable.

Like a structure designed to last indefinitely, community-based policing withstands destruction because of a strong, solid foundation. Sustained interpersonal communication and interaction between people in the police department and community and a friendly, open, outgoing attitude on the part of street police officers comprise the strength of desireable police community relations. Community-based policing consists of refined police community relations serving and meeting the policing needs of the community.

Community-based policing invariably produces effective policing because it relies on the only method ever known to consistently produce the desired results. Self-policing satisfies the community, without exception. Self-policing and community-based policing mean the same thing. Small towns and rural communities police best because they police themselves. They practice community-based policing.

Chapter 8

DISCRETION

POLICE *discretion* involves choosing a course of action from among legal alternatives. Police discretion never includes illegal choices. When police decide to employ an illegal method to handle a case, they decide to violate the law and do not utilize discretion. Officers selecting such an undertaking become criminals. They can no longer police effectively or fairly. Categorizing employees of police departments who commit crimes as police officers who display poor or no discretion serves only to erode public respect for police and corrode the true meaning of police discretion within police science. Before it can comprehend police discretion and how it works, the public must be educated to understand that officers who commit crimes do not use discretion when they break the law but rather officers who make judgement calls from legal alternatives do use police discretion.

Police *ethics* involves lying, deceit, perjury, theft, and other crimes perpetrated by police officers. It is a complex subject and beyond the scope of this book.

Since hindsight proves better than foresight, a critical concensus of opinion frequently follows any judgement call which was quickly made. But the fundamental nature of police work demands many hasty decisions, and circumstances do not always allow the officer sufficient time to progress properly through the decision-making process. Urgency may cause the officer to overlook one or more alternatives, it may not give the officer sufficient time to correctly weigh each alternative, or it may adversely influence the choice among considerations. Once the officer makes the decision and implements it, only the passage of time can accurately evaluate the propriety of police discretion.

Critics of a particular act of police discretion use terms like bad judgement, common sense, and poor discretion. The aviation adage, "any landing you can walk away from is a good landing," must contain some hidden, profound truth because it explains police discretion so well. Anytime all involved parties emerge from a police situation relatively unscathed, valid fair criticism of the police discretion used in that case becomes difficult to make. Only when someone suffers, figuratively or literally, as a result of police discretion can worthy and appropriate criticism emerge. Even then, criticism may meet frustration after realizing that limited time adversely influenced the decision. Limited time limits choices in policing.

Shoot-no-shoot scenarios present the most troublesome, difficult, and stressful discretion problems to police only because they all involve extremely limited time. If these incidents involved suffecient time, appellate courts and Monday morning quarterbacks as well as police officers would find life much more pleasant. But reality dictates otherwise. Close judgement calls form a cornerstone of policing as they do in baseball umpiring. Instant video replays authenticate the umpire's call when the pitch is clearly in or out of the strike zone. But when the ball passes within a hairbreath of that invisible line, the umpire does his job and makes a decision. That decision remains final regardless of what the replay shows.

Similarly, police make close, split second decisions. That is their job. Unfortunately, no instant video replays exist to help police learn and improve or to aid citizens in understanding police discretion. Conscientious police officers and umpires lose no sleep due to the way they employ discretion, regardless of the roar of critics. They know they did their best. The rewards of policing are personal. When an officer does his best in applying police discretion, he experiences all the feelings of contentment and satisfaction that accompany a job well done.

Studies of police discretion invariably commit that now familar research fallacy of generalization. Inductive reasoning excites more police myths than any other single factor except television. We forgive television since its purpose is to entertain, not educate. We cannot forgive writers who generalize when their goal is to educate, not entertain. The few studies that address police discretion involve researchers studying one or a few police departments. Observers record police practices and procedures, formal and informal, of officers in the field; analyze the data; and document the resulting conclusions.

Police discretion studies contain surprises for one whose knowledge of policing extends no further than television. The officers observed in these few studies conducted in large cities display considerably more latitude in police discretion than one might anticipate and definitely more than police administrators like to admit. Overlooking misdemeanors seems common, and permitting felonies and felons to go unrecorded appears as more than a rare occurrence. Some officers in large cities, when faced with a warrantless felony arrest decision, did not arrest in up to 50 percent of the cases. To those unfamiliar with police discretion, this might seem unthinkable. Three correlated factors explain this police action.

First, in the most noble of terms, the police goal remains justice. Second, police discretion includes only legal alternatives; but it does include all legal alternatives. Third, officers seldom view police department policy as powerful as the law or their goal of doing justice. Confronted on the street with a felony arrest situation and no witnesses, the officer and his partner frequently ignore police department policy to use police discretion. They decide, in this example, that justice is best served by not arresting. The fact that they violate police department policy, and thereby risk punishment, only strengthens the premise that they try to do justice. Few officers would not go to great lengths to jail a deserving asshole. My observations over the years indicate a great number of officers will invest significant time and effort to prevent anyone from being jailed if the officer believes justice would be better served in other ways. This includes such drastic measures as assuming risks by violating departmental policy. The officer violating police department policy in the interest of justice may lose a lot, but stands to gain only a sense of fairness and self-respect.

Any relationship existing between the results of police discretion and police department size remains largely unexamined with nationwide surveys and documentation. However, current knowledge of police discretion combined with what we know about small town and rural policing permit some limited but safe speculation. Small town communications, gossip, rumors, and the influential role the community plays in guiding and controlling the police seem certain to affect police discretion. Researchers may find that the officer on the large police department risks reprimand or suspension by the bureaucracy, but the officer on the small police department gambles with job security as a result of the same discretionary decision. What the officer may gain or lose as a result of a decision certainly affects every decision. Possible losses influence discretion. The bureaucracy permits greater error. The small town philosophy seems cold, unforgiving, and demanding at times.

The personal or acquaintance relationship found between officer and citizen with a greater frequency in small towns and rural communities probably also influences police discretion. Officers working the larger cities, in contrast, contact a relatively higher percentage of strangers which possibly affects officers' discretion. Small town and rural officers seem more likely to reencounter individuals they observe in police incidents. Realizing this possibility may influence the officer's discretion. The officer with the large police department likewise seems influenced by the belief that he will probably never see this person again.

A look at how police deal with domestic violence sheds some light on police discretion. The Crime Control Institute surveyed 176 police departments to determine how they preferred to handle domestic disputes. This study included no police departments with fewer than sixteen officers. Survey results place each police department in one of four categories: arrest, mediate, separate, and no policy.

According to that survey, more police departments indicate a preference for arresting as a disposition for domestic violence than for any of the other three. Mediation appears second and separation third. The bias of this particular survey reflects its listing no policy as the last category, and its labeling of this category. Many, perhaps most, of the police departments in the no policy category do practice and enforce a strong policy of officer discretion. These police departments rely on and trust the judgement of the officer in the field. They depend on the patrol officer to handle each case with the most appropriate disposition for that particular situation. These police departments do not tell their officers that every pitch will be a strike or a ball, but instead they expect officers to use discretion. This last group, with no policy, perhaps possesses the best policy of all, permitting police officers to police.

More accurately, two, not four, categories exist. One category prefers arresting, mediation, or separation over granting the officer discretion. This group attempts to call the pitches, before they are thrown, based on past pitches. The second believes in letting the umpire call the pitches. This group extends trust to the officer in the field in an attempt to police more effectively. They allow the officer to do the job, to make the judgement calls.

Based solely on the results of my surveys, which includes small town, rural, and large police departments in only two states, it appears that small town and rural police departments practice a policy of officer discretion more frequently than do large police departments. Bureaucracies prefer clear, objective guidelines to insure predictable results. Small town philosophy demands personal, subjective, individualized service. My interviews with scores of small town and rural chiefs and officers found not one who advocated policing family violence with a predetermined disposition. They seemed to agree that human behavior is not so cut and dried as to allow for prepackaged policing.

Perhaps no better example exists to illustrate how differently small and large police departments view discretion than their suggested approach to policing family violence. Bureaucracies establish and enforce detailed guidelines. If an officer encounters certain checklist items, policy dictates the officer must respond with a certain disposition. The bureaucracy polices by controlling the actions and reactions of the individual officer in the field. The bureaucracy cannot give the officer discretionary power because to do so would mean the bureaucracy relinquishes policing power to the individual. The patrol officer on the large police department acts not so much as a bureaucrat but as a mechanic for the bureaucracy.

In direct contrast, the small town philosophy relies on the individual officer to provide the full range of police services. Small towners and ruralites expect the officer to use and display discretion, make judgement calls, and police. They expect personal, individualized, custom designed policing. Small town philosophy mandates that all community members share in the responsibility for policing, but community members delegate the authority of police discretion to the police. The small town or rural community trusts the individual officer enough to expect him to use discretion. The patrol officer on the small town or rural police department acts not so much as a social mechanic but as a public servant.

Informal, unwritten policy can exert remarkable pressure on the decision-making process in police discretion. Such policies exist in many police departments without regard to size. What remains unknown, however, concerns how these informal, unwritten policies themselves vary by size of police department. Possibly the degrees of freedom granted the officer by this unwritten code correlate with police department size.

Ignorance about police discretion far exceeds knowledge of this intriguing and important subject. The fact that it is not what it seems to be remains the only thing we know for sure about police discretion. The fact that discretion remains intrinsic to policing means researching the former precedes understanding the latter. More research and study are sorely needed in this understudied area. Future research must include small town and rural police if accurate and complete pictures of police discretion result.

Chapter 9

TASKS ANALYSIS

THE PHILOSOPHY of a police department, the style of policing it practices, and the chemistry of the community determine police tasks and the time spent on individual tasks. No statistically significant relationship exists between what the police do, tasks; the time they spend performing a job, time on task; and the dependent variable, size of police department (see Appendix C).

Most police tasks analysis studies utilize one of two methodologies. They depend on observers to record and collect data, or they use the daily logs generated by the officers themselves.

Tasks analysis studies which rely on observers to record time on task seem to invariably contain a fatal flaw. Police officers possess no misconceptions about what they do and how long they spend on any task. However, reducing those two variables to valid and reliable statistics presents seemingly insurmountable hurdles. Police officers do possess, almost without exception, rather definite individual images of what they do that they want the public to see. The possibility of the observed individual changing behavior because of the presence of the observer always exists as a disadvantage to this method of data collection. In police tasks analysis studies this disadvantage looms so great that it often destroys the value of an otherwise superb study.

I require students in one of my courses to ride along with a police officer for the duration of an eight-hour shift. Hundreds of these students completed tasks analysis forms with police departments ranging in size from one officer to several thousand. Reliable evidence suggests many, and perhaps most, of these responses appear exaggerated beyond value. Some officers try hard to show the observer a good time, while others seem determined to give the student a taste of real police work. In an effort to recruit the student into a police career, a few officers try to sell

133

and promote the attractions of the job; while some do not enjoy the presence of a ride-along and go out of their way to bore or ignore the person, making it a miserable experience. Months after filing this anonymous data, one student confessed the officer falsified the entire response after they both spent eight hours watching TV in a fire department station.

The second method, using officer-generated daily logs, seems more reliable and valid; but several problems arise. Many police departments, of every size, do not require that officers complete a daily log to account for how and where they spend their time. As a result, many police departments do not possess the needed data. The practice of requiring officers to record and submit this information seems old fashioned to some police administrators and unnecessary to many others. When officers do prepare a daily log, they sometimes pad or distort information to satisfy the supervisor. In police departments that require these reports, officers often refer to them as "lie sheets."

Virtually all police tasks analysis studies reach one common conclusion. Police spend considerably less time than previously thought on tasks involving law enforcement, crime detection, identifying suspects, locating suspects, and the other tasks generally perceived as traditional, real police work. Neither do these studies control for the orientation of the police department among the six cells previously mentioned. Such oversight compromises any value of the study. These studies seem based on the erroneous premise that all police do the same things, an assumption which will prove fatal to any police study.

Future police tasks analysis studies must identify the police philosophy, the chemistry of the community, and the style of policing employed by the police department for the results to appear credible. Results of past studies seem to indicate generally a reactive philosophy and, perhaps, a watchman style. However, scholars should not rely on guesses or inductive reasoning. Past studies almost exclusively examined larger police departments. Future studies must identify the nature of the police department and the community for the results to prove valuable. Only then can researchers say with some accuracy that these police spend this amount of time on these tasks. Only then can researchers predict police tasks and time on tasks. The proper cell for a police department can be determined, and the amount of time spent on specific tasks predicted. Evidence currently available indicates no correlation exists between size of police department and tasks analysis.

Chapter 10

ADMINISTRATION, ORGANIZATION, AND RESOURCES

FREQUENTLY in the study of a particular subject, insight results from research into a tangent topic within the same field. Thus, we learn about people who are underweight by studying overweight people. To appreciate small town and rural police organization and administration, one must first grasp some basics of a bureaucracy. Education proceeds from the known, big town police departments, to the unknown, small town police departments. One can learn some of the things that make small town and rural police unique by first learning what they are not.

Are small town and rural police departments considered bureaucracies? Three ways exist to view a bureaucracy. The most common picture of a bureaucracy appears as a large, inefficient, uncaring, cold organization frozen with inactivity by its own red tape and snafus. The second approach reflects a sterile, remote, academic view where proponents claim to be objective and describe the bureaucracy in textbook terms of formal, ideal, visible characteristics. The final approach involves a combination of the first two and seems rare.

Four specific hallmark requirements define a bureaucracy: a division of labor, an authority structure, the distinct role and position of each member, and rules regulating relations between members.

A refined division of labor and specialization of tasks trademarks every bureaucracy. The larger a police department, the more specialization it will exhibit. Small town and rural police possess no specialization; they exist as generalists. After police department size reaches sixteen, specialization gradually emerges and increases until large police departments contain extensive specialization. Small town and rural police departments can claim little or no refined division of labor. In small community policing the chief may work as a patrol officer, the detective may make traffic stops, or the most recently hired officer may investigate crimes. Everyone on a small town or rural police department performs as generalists in a complete absence of specialization and division of labor. The responsibilities and duties of each officer's position remain neither precisely nor distinctly defined, making specialization impossible.

Larger police departments closely define, respect, and use an authority structure, while the same seems absent in the small town or rural police department. Larger police departments strictly follow a chain of command, claim formal relationships, and possess a military-like atmosphere. Smaller police departments seem characterized by informality, personal relationships, and a social, humanistic environment. Authority seems correlated to police department size; the larger the police department, the more authority incorporated. Any authority practiced in a small town or rural police department occurs because of respect and tradition, not because of enforced written regulations.

Larger police departments possess written distinct roles for each rank and position. In contrast, smaller police departments rely on informal, generalists roles, with each officer capable of fulfilling a variety of positions. Cross role performance seems the rule on small town police departments and the exception on big town police departments.

Larger police departments possess and observe more rules regulating relations between officers. Informality prevails on small town and rural police departments, but strict formality must rule on larger police departments (see Appendix E). On smaller police departments supervisors, ranking officers, and patrol officers appear more likely to use informal forms of address in interpersonal communication. They seem more likely to use titles and formal means of address on larger police departments. Roles at a crime scene or any police incident remain more likely to be clearly outlined in writing on larger police departments. Relations between officers on larger police departments seem colder, stilted, and less meaningful. The chain of command so strictly enforced on larger police departments inhibits and distorts communications, restricting relations between officers.

As the researcher observes increasingly larger police departments, more evidence of a bureaucracy becomes apparent. Bureaucracies seem best defined on a continuum and not categorically. Police departments employing fewer than sixteen armed officers rarely exhibit any of the four bureaucracy characteristics to any degree. Police departments claiming more than fifty to a hundred officers commonly demonstrate all four traits. Police departments with more than 150 to 200 officers usually illustrate all four traits to an advanced degree, and those few police departments with more than 500 officers often exemplify overbureaucratization.

The seemingly related subjects ignored by the four attributes illuminate small town and rural police organization and administration. The definition of a bureaucracy contains no mention of goals or objectives. Larger police departments proudly display their goals, such as "to protect and serve." This serves as window dressing to reassure a frightened public. The singular *de facto* goal of any bureaucracy remains self-perpetuation with growth, power maintenance and increasing the power base. Machiavelli described this phenonmenon five hundred years ago. Bureaucracies claim many and various stated goals, often very honorable and noble sounding; but the only real goal of any bureaucracy appears self-serving. Bureaucracies do not wither away and die. They grow bigger, stronger, and more powerful and impersonal. Like a corporation, each bureaucracy assumes a personality and a distinct entity. It is born and it grows.

A ball bearing manufacturing plant in Germany during World War II was located miles away from its administrative offices. Relentless bombing totally destroyed the plant itself, but no one informed the home office, so they continued doing business as usual. A war raged and it rolled smoothly along on ball bearings. For many months afterwards the home office filled orders, received orders, processed invoices, verified shipments, monitored production, kept books, and continued to function in the finest, most efficient bureaucratic tradition. Bureaucracies continue in good health without purpose.

The largest and most successful organizations in the world today exist as bureaucracies. They assume many responsibilities, thus freeing individuals for other endeavors. Bureaucratic inefficiency and ineffectiveness appear legendary, but for organizing and controlling large masses of people, bureaucracies remain far superior to all other alternatives.

Small town and rural police seem the antithesis of bureaucrats. Organization and administration of small or rural community police departments guide them as informal, personal, caring, and human; possessing and exhibiting *de facto* goals of delivering a wide range of services to their communities. Small town and rural officers police by performing community designated tasks to the satisfaction of the community. Large police departments develop their own entity; and officers establish a relationship with that entity—a lopsided relationship that frequently causes the officer to act with a blind, unquestioned faith. Small town and rural police departments, unable to establish their own entity, adopt and share the collective wholeness of the community. The police department acts as a vital part of the community, while the officer establishes many relationships throughout the community. These relationships seem balanced, equal, reciprocal, complementary, and healthy.

Efficiency and effectiveness appear as two common bureaucratic terms. Efficiency means the most waste-free utilization of energy, time, money, and resources. Effectiveness refers to the proportion of goals that seem reached. The vehicle that travels thirty miles on one gallon of gas operates more efficiently than the vehicle traveling ten miles on two gallons. If a traveler plans to arrive in a distant city for an important appointment, his efforts seem effective when he arrives on time. This example illustrates that the two do not always relate. Either may exist without the other; they may coexist, or correlate.

The small town or rural officer sitting in a local restaurant conversing with locals for three hours uses resources more efficiently than the megacity officer riding with a partner in an air conditioned car in and out of stop and go traffic for three hours. The small town or rural officer builds trust, confidence, and a personal bond between citizens and the police, all indicators of effective policing. The wise budget-minded chief uses the gallons of burned gas, miles of vehicle depreciation, and hours of patrol time to justify and expand the bureaucracy. To perpetuate and expand the bureaucracy remain the only goals of Megacity Police Department, and to that end the two cool officers contribute efficiently and effectively. However, only the small town or rural officer polices, and only the small town or rural officer polices with any degree of effectiveness.

The only goal of small town and rural police remains policing the community in a manner acceptable to all people in the community. A chief of a big city police department who organizes or administers with a goal not compatible and consistent with the bureaucracy will not last long. A small town or rural chief attempting to police the community in any way other than what the people desire will soon exist without gainful employment.

Stated goals of big city police departments never coincide with defacto goals. On small town and rural police departments stated goals and defacto goals generally seem congruent. On any police department with more than one officer, an informal power structure may run and control police department operations. The chief of a police department may exist as only a symbolic figurehead, while a small but very powerful group actually direct and manage the police department. Depending upon the goals of the informal group, this can prove beneficial, or harmful, to improving policing.

Growth of an informal power structure may appear quick and revolutionary or slow and almost undetectable at first. The former seems more likely to fail, but it usually involves more drastic change when it does succeed. An alert chief will detect such a movement early, identify the instigators, and neutralize the insurgency. Generally, the more drastic the means of quelling the uprising, the more effective they seem. Intelligent officers realize the extreme risks involved with establishing informal organizations and therefore engage in them only when feeling desperate. When they believe there remains nothing to lose, officers seriously consider running the police department themselves.

On those police departments controlled by an informal power structure, the chief remains but a figurehead. The figurehead chief chooses one of two roles. Some chiefs appear like the drum major, ignorant of the parade route, who slows at each intersection, glances over a shoulder, and then rushes to stay in front and lead the parade. The tail wags the dog. Other figurehead chiefs seem happy with their bogus role and drift along with the current as worthless flotsam.

If the goals of the informal power structure serve to improve policing, then the community benefits. But if the goals serve only the selfish interests of the informal leaders, then the community and policing suffer.

An informal group can become a powerful and moving change agent on any police department. Because of tremendous bureaucratic momentum inherent in large police departments, more energy seems necessary to establish an informal administration on a large police department than on a small police department. Additionally, bureaucracies contain numerous built-in safeguards to discourage and disarm takeover attempts. Only when informal administrations serve the ends of the bureaucracy better than do formal administrations, can the informal leaders survive. An informal administration will replace the formal one in a bureaucracy only when the informal structure makes the bureaucracy more bureaucratic.

Since informal power groups require less start-up energy on small town and rural police departments and since no bureaucracy exists, informal administrations that produce improved policing occur with greater frequency in smaller towns. These informal administrations that result in improved policing act as change agents. They manage to break the cement of tradition and deliver police services which satisfy a larger fraction of the community.

Frequently, the community sees only the figurehead chief and falsely assumes the improvement results from the chief's actions. The informal administration delights in watching the chief receive credit for something someone else accomplished.

The leader of such a movement often succeeds as a change agent who multiplys efforts; the individual's goals become the group's goals. One person improves the policing of an entire police department. One person, with a fitting attitude and determination, can easily improve policing from a chief's position. Any street officer can improve policing—one person can make a difference.

Effective work groups, whether formal or informal, always consist of psychological groups. In contrast, a psychological group does not always make an effective work group. A psychological group seems limited in size to fifteen. Psychological groups possess personalities: average or dull, slow or quick, cheerful or gloomy, etc. Like individuals, psychological groups may possess goals.

When the goals of the individual do not coincide with those of the group, the psychological group will tend to ostracize or expel the individual. When the individual's goals seem concurrent with the group's goals, the individual becomes an effective group member.

Now, consider the group's goals. Each psychological group possesses its own personality and goals. If these goals seem consistent with remaining tasks or with the bureaucracy's goals, the group will probably become an effective work group. If the goals seem inconsistent, it cannot develop into an effective work group.

Small town and rural police departments existing as effective work groups seem relatively more common than larger police departments that contain effective work groups. Larger police departments seldom reach goals of effective policing but virtually always succeed in effectively reaching goals of the bureaucracy. Small town and rural police frequently obtain goals of effective policing but contribute nothing to a bureaucratic process.

Organization and administration include those activities and efforts which assist a police department in obtaining its objectives. Organization includes, but is not limited to, planning, staffing, supervision, control, coordination, organizing, communications, and budgeting. Administration involves the application of leadership to organization. Although every police department seems a child of the constituency it serves, in a more immediate and practical sense, the chief determines the policing style and philosophy of a police department. This aids understanding why the chief appears the single most important person on any police department, large or small. The only exception remains the police department with only a figurehead chief controlled by an informal power structure.

For effective policing, any police chief should claim a background in various aspects of police work in addition to possessing the many traits of a competent and proficient leader. Often smaller towns and cities set themselves up for numerous future problems by selecting a person with no police experience to serve as police chief. A new chief should inherit the responsibility and authority of the position. Responsibility means accountability while authority implies the right and power to act. In a healthy police environment the chief must possess both.

Whether a municipality claims a strong or weak mayor form of government, the chief must practice open communications with the mayor, city manager, and council members to experience success. The chief must strive to establish and maintain open and free communication channels with all other individuals in city government, including other department heads. Often this requires the chief going more than half way. Compromise seldom includes equal give and take. The chief who goes out of his way to socialize over coffee occasionally with the finance director will probably not regret it during the annual budget preparation. The hardware, trappings, and atmosphere of a police department intimidate some. The wise chief recognizes these factors and compensates to maintain good objective working relationships with the people who manage city government.

An applicant for a police chief position on a small town or rural police department should meet individually with the mayor, city manager, and each council member, if possible. This will alert the applicant to potential personality clashes or major differences in police philosophies or styles. Such private meetings might also forewarn the applicant that city government clings to unrealistic expectations of its police. Conversely, city government representatives can better evaluate the applicant. If after meeting with each of these individuals, the applicant feels confidant and comfortable with the apparent communications channels, then no insurmountable hurdles should arise for the new chief.

Being in the business of helping those who ask for help, police officers develop a strong reluctance to ask for help themselves. The successful small town or rural chief remains the one who learns to break the mad cycle and ask for help. He seeks help in becoming a team member and cultivating membership on the police department team, the city management team, and in the community spirit between the police department and the people.

Establishing effective communications from the onset, even before one begins employment as chief, with an attitude of willingness to converse, listen, and help, appears the surest way to maintain positive, productive communications.

Many small town and rural chiefs speak longingly of more job security in the form of a written contract. In reality such appears rare. During the hiring phase a clear written agreement serves to clarify expectations of both parties. Such an agreement should outline the chief's rights, including the right to notice of charges, reasonable time to answer the charges, and a right to a public hearing concerning the charges. Asking for this agreement is not unreasonable. Requiring this agreement usually remains the applicant's choice. A person accepting a chief's job after the city refuses to reduce such fundamental rights to writing at least knows the risks he assumes with the job. A written statement of the small town or rural chief's rights helps insure that a chief will not suffer unjust termination while at the same time insuring that a community can rid itself of an incompetent police executive.

Increased and less whimsical job security for the chief seems another advantage of big city police departments. Bureaucracies offer the attraction of protecting their own, especially those higher up in the organization like the police chief.

The chief executive, whether chief or sheriff, of a small town or rural community remains indisputably the most important single individual on that police department. Just as no guaranteed formula for success in policing exists, no known formula emerges promising success to the chief. Leadership styles vary among chiefs; and, because individual personality remains a part of leadership, management styles vary among small town and rural police executives. The 254 sheriff's offices in Texas include approximately 254 management styles.

However, most management styles clearly fall into one of two categories, *reactive* and *progressive*. Reactive styles seem satisfied with tradition, while progressive styles often display initiative and a willingness to change.

Management by objectives seems a typical progressive style. Management by objectives means a system that determines objectives and establishes a plan to accomplish objectives. It provides an ideal business like approach. It gives police a goal which tends to increase morale and influence enthusiasm. Management by objectives requires measureable objectives, frequent assessment, self-criticism, and constant evaluation and correction, it seldom seems easy. Perhaps these same requirements make progressive management less attractive to small town and rural police executives.

Fundamental hallmark characteristics that make small town and rural policing unique seem difficult or impossible to measure. High quality interaction between an officer and a citizen in a small town presents enormous measurement problems. Aspects of policing or leadership that lend themselves to measurement and assessment appear similar or identical to those facets of policing or leadership easily counted. Since small town and rural policing emphasizes quality over quantity, management by objectives does not always work ideally in those settings. Because bureaucracies tend to value quantity over quality, management by objectives frequently works well when applied in a bureaucracy.

Management by objectives contains powerful basic administration principles which few successful chiefs ignore. Setting objectives and priorities, planning, and following a plan seem characteristic of most effective police executives. Strong, effective police leadership usually results in healthy, effective policing. Weak, ineffective leadership causes unpredictable policing.

The goals and objectives of some small town and rural police departments remain unconsidered and never discussed. Usually this results in *status-quo* policing — no experimentation, no innovation, and little or no improvement. The wise small town or rural chief constantly stays abreast of developments and community goals and expectations by maintaining clear communications channels with city administration and citizens. This enables the chief to accurately estimate what the community expects from its police. Like a thirty-year sheriff, the successful small town or rural chief remains mindful of the mood of the people. A sheriff worries about reelection once every two or four years, the small town or rural chief may worry about future job security constantly.

Proactive policing involves progressive policing. The proactive chief instills in officers a sincere desire to maximize the number of observations of and interventions in the community. Although proactive policing often produces increased arrests on larger police departments, proactive policing in small towns and rural communities frequently results in improved police community relations, not in increased arrests. Proactive policing includes reactive policing, but proponents argue that over an extended period the crime prevention efforts will significantly reduce the reactive policing workload. A good chief can make this happen.

Searching, experimenting, risking, improvising, and advancing policing: the progressive chiefs bear responsibility for the many worthwhile innovations in policing today. These chiefs risk a lot, humilation and failure, for a chance to gain a better way to police. Some fortunate chiefs enjoy such security that they risk little when they experiment big. These few chiefs can do no wrong. Overall, the innovative chief, regardless of police department size, deserves recognition and respect for improving policing in the United States.

A seemingly endless assortment of different types of reactive police administration exists. The one made famous by the mass media seems the most common: this police executive completes the absolutely essential and nothing more. No news is good news. A day spent asleep behind the desk or reading sex magazines appears a good day. To this chief, the officer making a traffic stop asks for trouble. Anytime this chief seems busy, he deals only with reactions. The day-to-day busy work of running an office occupies all this chief's time.

The chief who manages by procrastination frustrates officers even more. Police work is action, the antithesis of procrastination. The procrastinating chief learns that delay may remove the responsibility of a wrong decision. No decision becomes the safest choice. Not uncommon on small town and rural police departments, this chief seems a bureaucrat without a bureaucracy, a captain without a ship. He develops expertise in appointing study groups, committees, and assigning individual officers, who feel highly complimented but never realize their recommendations remain unread. Though frequently an expert in disguising procrastination, this chief remains completely ineffective.

Erskine Caldwell described a sheriff who hung a "gone fishin' " sign on his office door and disappeared when any case or controversy developed. Police remain the short stop for the troubles of our society. They handle situations which no one else can or will. Avoidance of a problem by a police chief or sheriff seems nothing less than negligence of duty and serves only to aggravate the community's troubles. Numerous small town and rural chiefs told me they prefer to stay out of sight. Out of sight out of mind. Such mentality recognizes that all ships are safe in a harbor but fails to acknowledge that is not what ships are for. A disappearing chief selfishly survives while contributing nothing to helping the community. Such a chief often seems counterproductive, doing more harm than good.

Unlike the military with its mission and unlike profit motive organizations, the goals of policing remain unclear. The chief must outline for the officers objectives acceptable to city management and the community. Likewise, the chief must project the leadership necessary to foster harmonious efforts towards accomplishing the goals. The chief dictates the style of policing employed in a community and generates the atmosphere and philosophy for working policing officers. A police department remains no place for one to rise to a level of incompentency. The best administrator working as chief, the best supervisor supervising, and the best police officers on the street policing constitute the ideal.

No management style or program of any police department should be labeled a failure if it brings the police department and the community closer together. No administration or program can be labeled a success if it increases the distance, in any way, between the police and the citizens.

The actual organizational structure of a small town or rural police department remains a function of the number of officers employed and the number of hours per week that the agency provides services. It surprises many to learn that some police departments do not provide 24-hour service, seven days a week. A small town or rural police department with fewer than five officers cannot provide around-the-clock services with each person working only a 40-hour week. Considering 168 hours in a week divided by forty equals 4.2, five officers remain necessary to provide 24-hour services.

Many reason that since a 24-hour period contains three 8-hour shifts, only three shifts appear necessary. This would work great if officers never took a day off and weekends required no policing. The joys of struggling with a duty roster teach otherwise. Off days require a fourth shift or its equivalent.

A police department with three, seven, or fifteen officers seems ideal in terms of span of control. Span of control means the number of persons reporting to one supervisor, and the number of persons one supervisor can effectively manage. This number varies with the supervisory abilities of the individual, seldom including more than two or three and almost never more than five or six subordinates. Successful, effective chiefs recognize that some cannot supervise more than one other, and some simply cannot supervise. The wise chief knows the officers' abilities and organizes accordingly. A police department with seven or fifteen officers lends itself to easy structuring so that no one supervises more than two others. Many larger police departments organize so that one sergeant may supervise seven or more officers. This arrangement seems ridiculous and expects the impossible. The individual capable of supervising effectively more than four or five subordinates remains extremely rare.

Rank seems important on small town and rural police departments and correlates to span of control, morale, and other leadership principles. Rank appears needed to clarify lines of authority and to streamline the organizational framework, even on the smallest of police departments. Some police departments with two officers find it beneficial with the second officer ranked a patrol officer; while the experience of other police departments requires the second officer ranked a sergeant. The same applies on a police department of three. The chief must determine whether to organize with one or two sergeants, or two patrol officers.

A police department with four officers seems best organized with one first-line supervisor (sergeant and lieutenant appear the most frequently used ranks) and two patrol officers. This arrangement frees the chief to supervise one instead of three. This size police department can provide around-the-clock policing with only one 8-hour shift per week not covered. Usually the chief covers the day shift Monday through Friday, with the one open shift occuring on the day shift either Saturday or Sunday. A reserve officer or the chief may work that period. A chief working the street each Saturday will probably accomplish more meaningful police community relations in one Saturday than in all the other days combined.

The wise small town or rural chief also uses Sunday to strengthen police community bonds. Policing tends to bleach religion out of some officers by forcing them to witness enormous amounts of human suffering, deprivation, and criminals intentionally hurting innocent victims. Unable to resolve for themselves how so much pain and suffering can exist with a Supreme Being, they lose faith. Nevertheless, the politically astute police chief and the long-tenured sheriff attend religious services in their jurisdictions with some regularity. Some citizens will otherwise never see their police chief, or any police officer. Such social intercourse encourages healthy relationships as it helps the chief maintain a proper perspective and avoid cynicism. In small towns and rural communities the church remains a significant social institution, a fact not wasted to the wise police chief.

A police department with five officers does not face the scheduling difficulties confronting police departments with fewer officers. A police department of five might organize with one or two sergeants, or one sergeant and one lieutenant. This organization permits the chief to work patrol one shift per week.

All officers on small town and rural police departments are generalists. Virtually all small town or rural chiefs perform as street chiefs, not desk chiefs. Reality mandates they work as a composite of two extremes. The chief of a police department with five officers can in theory work thirty-two hours a week in administration and eight hours on the street. In reality this chief spends considerably more time on the street and in the community. Some experts on small group dynamics consider five the ideal size.

Discussion thus far ignores sick days and vacation time. No modern-day small town or rural chief can afford to ignore this issue. Sick days, vacations, and compensatory time create overtime on small town and rural police departments. On a five-member police department, if one takes vacation and another calls in sick, no one remaining will receive off days until either the vacationing or sick officer returns. Even if the budget permits paying overtime this may cause a strain on those concerned. Sometimes resolutions to these problems do not exist for the small town or rural chief.

A total of six officers seems the minimum needed to run a 24-hour operation with allowances for sick, vacation, and compensentory time. Even with six officers, scheduling problems arise. Like all other employees, police officers seem to pick the worst possible time to call in sick. One tenet of Murphy's law states that if something can go wrong, it will, at the worst possible time. Again, these remain some of the unavoidable problems of small town and rural police administration. Bureaucracies do not suffer these situations.

As a review of police department organization and administration by size of police department proceeds, a police department with six appears the first which, in theory, does not require the chief to work anytime on patrol. The sixth position should add a patrol position to the organization, not a ranking position.

Appendix B illustrates possible rank distribution and organizational schemes for small town and rural police departments. These appear only as models based on certain organizational and administrative principles. Appendix B, understandably, does not include all possibilities. More than two levels must never exist between top and bottom; small town and rural police departments must never include more than four levels in their organizational structure. Face to face interaction remains a unique advantage of small town and rural police departments. Introducing a third level between the chief and the patrol officer serves to add dangerous distance and aloofness to the chief and rapidly destroys the personal atmosphere. Formalities and hints of a bureaucracy appear with more than two levels between top and bottom.

Maintaining at least half the personnel at patrol officer rank seems desirable. This prevents a police department from becoming rank heavy. Span of control appears as a third principle demonstrated in the illustration. No one supervises more than three. Span of control remains a powerful concept and should be respected even at the expense of violating another principle. For example, in a police department of five, if no one seems capable of supervising more than two others, the chief should reform with two sergeants and two patrol officers.

Because of unavoidable difficulties in scheduling and because the very nature of police work dictates officers work relatively unsupervised, on small town and rural police departments supervision acquires new meaning. Here it seems common for a patrol officer to work for weeks, or indefinitely, without a supervisor assigned to the same shift. Moving from the neat, simple organizational charts in the illustration to scheduling shift assignments remains difficult and awkward at best. The patrol officer may work a shift alone or with another of the same rank. A sergeant may work alone with no one to supervise. On an established schedule this may create surprisingly few problems.

On a small town or rural police department rank serves purposes other than lines of authority. Rank serves as prestige, reward, and recognition for experience, seniority, merit, or all three. Rank lends a framework to the group and can contribute greatly to morale.

Many small town or rural officers consider seven the perfect size police department. Seven remains the group size in which the average person feels at ease with that many face-to-face relationships. Seven offers a neat structure with two sergeants each overseeing two patrol officers.

With the addition of the eighth position the chief must decide whether to add another level, as in the illustration, or add another patrol officer. Examination of the illustration indicates that as the size of the police department increases, more organizational arrangements emerge. The size of five overcomes the problem of the chief working the street forty hours, or more, a week; six means the chief may try to lead from behind a desk and not worry about vacation, sick leave, and overtime; and seven or more officers adds increased comfort to the chief's administrative and organizational efforts.

Fielding two officers around the clock, compensating for vacations, sick days and compensatory time without paying overtime, requires fifteen officers. Occasionally maintaining only one officer on duty provides the cushion necessary for these small town and rural police luxuries.

Temptation to conclude that bigger is better arises. Extended study, however, of police community relations experienced almost exclusively on small town and rural police departments enables understanding to overcome temptation. As police department size increases, scheduling difficulties decrease and disappear; but community policing difficulties increase and become paramount.

A fifteen officer police department projects the appearance of few scheduling problems, certainly fewer than the police department with only three or four officers. Consequently, some reason that twenty officers would be better and forty twice as good as twenty. On a shift schedule, more is better. In the real world of policing, smaller seems better. In the United States today thousands of police departments with fewer than five officers respond to calls around the clock and provide quality, effective police services to their communities.

Small town and rural officers enjoy pointing out that if their police department size were doubled, it would not result in a doubling of police effectiveness. Police officers seem a proud lot, but small town and rural officers take a special pride in their employing agency. Small town and rural police help police scientists realize that more officers will never substitute for better policing. They remind others that in policing, quality, not quantity, measures effectiveness.

The organization and administration of small town and rural police departments produce interesting managerial concepts. An understanding of *police ratio, patrol payroll ratio, patrol deployment,* and *patrol density* seems a prequisite to any appreciation of the differences between small and big town policing.

Police ratio, the number of armed officers per 1,000 citizens, seems the most fitting measure for determining the appropriate size of a police department. Administrators frequently use police ratio comparisons with other police departments to justify an increase in the number of officers allocated their police department. If all, or even most, police officers policed, this would work well; but someone must run the store.

Police ratios vary from less than one officer per 1,000 citizens to six or seven officers per 1,000 citizens. On a nationwide average, larger police departments claim more officers per 1,000 citizens than small town and rural police departments do. Police ratio also give a false impression that big city residents receive more for their police tax dollars. As every officer knows, appearances deceive.

Patrol payroll ratio, the percentage of the total officers on a police department assigned to patrol, strongly correlates with the size of the police department. The smaller the police department, the greater will be the percentage of officers assigned to patrol. Police departments with 150 or more seldom assign more than 50 or 60 percent of their officers to patrol. The largest police departments, those with more than 1,000 officers, usually assign less than 50 percent to patrol. Organizing and administrating a large bureaucracy requires and consumes many people. Someone must complete the tons of paperwork for those millions and billions of ball bearings.

Patrol payroll ratio receives no attention or publicity. The mediacracy reassures us that all police officers spend their time on the street policing. Police administrators on larger police departments understandably hesitate to discuss it openly since they may then appear as inept managers.

For many decades "The Greatest Show on Earth," the Ringling Brothers and Barnum and Bailey Circus, provided transportation and room and board to more than 1,000 extra circus roustabouts whose only job involved putting up and taking down the tent each time the circus moved. New owners brought innovative organization and administration which revolutionized the circus world. Tenting was abandoned in favor of convention centers, coliseums, and indoor circuses. For the first time in history performers outnumbered roustabouts. Attendance and profits soared dramatically.

Many police departments cling desperately to bureaucratic traditions, insisting on the unnecessary waste of valuable resources, reasoning that a circus is not a circus without a tent.

Many assume that all officers assigned to patrol literally work on the street policing. Patrol deployment represents the percentage of officers in the police department (or on the payroll) on the street at certain times (10:00AM and 10:00PM, for example). This seems a more accurate measure since only about one fourth of officers on larger police departments appear on duty at any given time, since only about one-half of those work in patrol, and since some in patrol do not work the streets. As the personnel strength of a police department decreases, the percentage of those officers working the street increases. As police department size increases, the proportion of officers assigned positions other than patrolling the streets increases.

The combined action of patrol payroll ratio and patrol deployment means that as police department size decreases, the percentage of its officers on the street policing at any given time increases (see Appendix F). Small town and rural police departments seem more able to translate people on the payroll to police on the street. Small town and rural police redefine police ratio. With fewer officers on the payroll per 1,000 citizens, they manage to put more officers on the street policing per 1,000 citizens.

Patrol density means the number of police officers on the street per 1,000 citizens. Once again the absence of a bureaucracy accounts for small town and rural police exhibiting the most desirable. As police department size decreases the number of police on the street per 1,000 citizens increases (see Appendix F). If citizens pay taxes expecting their local government to provide services by putting police out in the community, then the smaller the city, the greater the citizens' return on their investment (see Appendix G). A friend living in a middle class section of Houston saw no police cars pass his house or even in his neighborhood in eight-plus years. I live in a town of less than 8,000 and frequently see a patrol unit cruise by my home. Viewed through police eyes, each officer on the streets of a larger city must police more people.

Although big city police departments employ more officers per 1,000 citizens than do smaller cities, the latter fields more officers per 1,000 citizens than does the former. If administrative effectiveness and organizational efficiency means converting police on the payroll, or police ratios, to police on the street serving citizens, then small town and rural police departments prove themselves more effective and efficient. The absence of a bureaucracy, its organizers and administrators, and the relative small numbers account for increased effectiveness and efficiency on small town and rural police departments.

Most small town and rural police departments do not possess a written policy manual. Virtually all large police departments issue a copy of their written guidelines to each officer. These books outline policies, procedures, and expectations in a guideline format for the officer to follow. Subject matter varies from personal grooming standards to booking procedures to attempts at making discretionary decisions for the officer.

In small town and rural police departments the absence of written policy acts to the advantage of the administrator and the disadvantage of the street officer. The chief plays it by ear. The chief can always claim an officer's judgement or discretion contrary to established departmental policy. In contrast the officer on the street possesses no policy to assist in decisions or support the officer's actions. Too frequently this results not with the officer policing appropriately but with the officer policing to keep the chief happy.

The modern, effective chief does everything within his power to help the officer on the street. At a bare minimum this includes development and continuous refinement of written department policy. A well researched, clear, concise policy manual serves the best interests of all involved and paves the way to better policing.

The modern, effective chief utilizes organization and administration and endless interaction with the community to lead his police department in improving policing. These chiefs, who exist on all size police departments, lead by setting an example, displaying initiative, and practicing proper supervision. They emphasize training, education, and all forms of self improvement, knowing that improving individual officers will quickly improve policing. They never hesitate to join the community in any effort or program which offers any promise, no matter how slim, of creating more effective policing. Lastly, they all seem to understand that no effort or program can be labeled a total failure if it causes police and citizens to interact.

Limited economics and frugal budgets create a restricted environment for the majority of small town and rural police. The small town or rural police chief frequently operates with daily problems unknown to chiefs of larger police departments. These problems invariably seem caused by economics. Problems of policing faced by the street officer seem universal and vary only with the nature or chemistry of the people. The greatest problems confronting large police departments involve groups of people and seldom concern money. The greatest problems facing small town and rural police departments seldom concern people but seemingly always involve money. Large police departments enjoy a comfortable economic base, while small town and rural police must remain content with a base made of people. Bureaucracies seem more oriented towards economics and tangible resources, while in contrast small groups seem more people-oriented.

Perhaps nowhere in policing does the idea that "bigger is better" demonstrate more validity than in economics. The budgets of large police departments appear disproportionately large. Just as a strong positive correlation exists between police department size and officers' salaries, a significant difference occurs between police department size and the amount of the annual budget. Police departments with one hundred times more officers than a small town or rural police department will claim a budget 150 or even 200 times larger. Salary differences do not explain such variances (see Appendix E).

The percentage of officers required to run the police department and occupy nonpolice positions increases from about 10 percent on a police department with ten officers to about 50 percent of a fifty officer department, subsequently leveling off. A similar phenomenon occurs with police budgets, except no ceiling exists.

Salaries account for the greatest single cost of any police department's budget. The percentage of the budget for nonsalary items increases from a low of 5 to 10 percent on small town and rural police departments to a high of 40 percent or more on the largest police departments. No leveling off appears. The bigger the police department, the more people and money needed to operate the bureaucracy. Small group dynamics (a redundant phrase since large group dynamics do not exist) compensate, even to the point that a few small town or rural police departments claim nothing in their budgets for nonsalary items. Salaries, or salary, comprise the total budget. A few small town or rural police departments budget for nonsalary items only every second or every third year. Imagine the money larger police departments would save if they adopted such a practice. Circumstances force small town and rural police departments to cut corners and save money. The nature of bureaucracies dictates certain waste; sincere efforts to save money seem anti-bureaucratic. Bureaucracies eat money and have nothing to show for it, in the police world, except fat; frequently washed new police cars; and bullet resistant, clear plastic shields.

Many items that receive considerable budget attention on larger police departments, such as training, technology improvements, and narcotics and vice operations, receive little or no money in small town and rural police budgets. Contingency accounts infrequently appear on the budgets of smaller police departments. A few small town detectives and chiefs must convince the city manager, or worse, the finance director, of the necessity of each long distance telephone call.

The parent organization, the municipal or county government, seems most frequently the explanation for a bare-bones budget. No evidence exists suggesting that these bodies discriminate unfairly against police departments. They give each department a restricted budget. Police salaries of small town and rural officers seem lower by comparison to other officers not because of agency size but because of small town and rural economics. Small town teachers, doctors, lawyers, and plumbers earn less than their big city counterparts. Likewise, the limited budgets of small town and rural police departments seem explained at least in part by the economics of their umbrella organizations. Small town and rural utility, fire, and maintenance departments receive disproportionally less in budgets than their metroplex siblings.

A chief's lack of sophistication in all budget matters also explains unreasonable budgets in too many small town and rural police departments. Chiefs of larger police departments more frequently possess the expertise, experience, and confidence required to plan, present, and justify an appropriate budget. Wise police chiefs anticipate and prepare for budget hearings with the dedication and determination of a general making ready for war. The street provides the stage for the officer to demonstrate proficiency, and budget hearings give the best opportunity for the chief to chief and show his mettle. Superb chiefs often receive superb budgets, whereas chicken manure chiefs usually receive chicken feed budgets.

Officers retiring from careers on large police departments sometimes seek chief positions on small town and rural police departments as retirement havens. This proves beneficial to the tired and retired chief and detrimental to policing and all other persons involved. This person usually appears as a retired police officer in chief's clothing who knows little and cares less about budgeting. Typically such a person discovered years prior that cursing the darkness seems easier than lighting a candle. Far too many chiefs complain all year about the budget but then make no effort to improve the situation for next year.

Most small town and rural police departments claim no expertise or confidence in grant writing and proposals. Bureaucracies make special allowances permiting certain persons to work full time developing grants. It now seems almost indisputable that larger police departments receive a disproportionately large share of the grant pie. No solution seems to exist to rectify this imbalance. If they want free money, small town and rural chiefs must identify any person with grantsmanship skills or potential and encourage and help that person. Not all small town and rural police departments want free money. They seem convinced that free money includes too many attached strings and conditions. Conservative by nature, many of these administrators believe free money does not exist except as more bureaucratic doublespeak.

What small town and rural police departments lack in budgets, they make up in innovation. What they lack in resources and facilities, they compensate with resourcefulness and determination. They use human qualities and characteristics in policing in the absence of money and hardware. They police people with people, not with opulence.

Resources and physical facilities of large police departments never vary in terms of adequacy. The same building houses the Berkeley, California Police Department today that housed it fifty years ago. Imperfect then, it remains adequate today. Large police departments carefully monitor on video each movement of every entrant into their sterile world but refuse to even try to help the citizens so stupid as to lock the keys inside their own cars. Resources and physical facilities of small town and rural police departments vary in terms of adequacy from the more than sufficient to the comical to the dangerously inadequate.

Small town or rural police departments with workable, adequate budgets and resources enjoy the best of both worlds, providing the most efficient and effective policing possible. Small town or rural police departments cursed with inadequate resources and facilities improvise with human determination and small group dynamics.

Police vehicles prove, perhaps, the most troublesome area of nonsalary items. The cushion, the percentage of vehicles available for repairs, maintenance, and use as spares, increases as police department size increases. Many small town and rural police departments run their entire fleet constantly, 24 hours a day. This practice seems the fastest way to depreciate vehicles. When one vehicle breaks down, another works twice as hard.

The humor employed by an individual or group often reveals great insight into that person or group. Officers employed by big cities seem to joke more about human tragedy and less about resources. A car that balks when the throttle is suddenly opened or idles rough remains serious business and cause to cease all activity and exchange vehicles. These officers need a near perfect car to police. In contrast, small town and rural police appear to joke more about fiscal shortcomings and resources and less about human suffering and victimization. If the vehicle will transport, that's good enough, for after all, that is all any of them will do.

A small town police department in Southern Louisiana made the Associated Press wire service after all five patrol cars failed to make it to any of three robberies that occurred in one hour. Call number one came in during shift change and two officers immediately jumped in one car to respond. It failed to start. Their recovery seemed instant. Out of one and into number two, which also failed to start. Out of two, into three. Strike three, it refused to start. Relentless in their pursuit of justice, they wisely jumped into one of the officer's personal vehicles and answered the call. Robbery call number two came in and the chief could not start his vehicle. Another officer flagged a ride to the scene with a passing motorist. Of the two patrol cars which eventually departed for the scene, one died and had to be restarted with jumper cables, while the other suffered a flat tire but hobbled along to within running distance of the robbery. Undaunted, the officers recovered and responded to robbery call number three, arriving in time for a fire fight that wounded an officer, the robber, and a clerk. The chief pointed out that all the vehicles were operated around the clock. The chief previously requested the city council to provide tools so the officers might repair and service the vehicles.

Many small town and rural police departments report officers performing routine maintenance and repair on police vehicles. All police departments with take home car programs experience better vehicle maintenance and extended service. Perhaps some small town and rural police departments without permanently assigned vehicles but with circumstances permitting officers to routinely take vehicles home would also experience improved vehicle upkeep.

A small town police department in Massachusetts lost its only police vehicle when the car failed the state safety inspection. It is frightening to wonder how many small town and rural police vehicles bear false inspection stickers. Other police departments lose all their vehicles to wrecks or too many hard, fast miles. When this happens, small town and rural officers improvise. They use vehicles from other city departments when feasible. When painted into a corner, officers drive their own vehicles. Sometimes this happens with reimbursement, but often-times it takes the form of a personal contribution to the cause. In a few rare cases these officers must resort to policing without a vehicle. Ironically, the officer finds himself forced into a walking foot patrol, the essence of policing.

Until the mid-eighties, the Sheriff's Office in Newport, Arkansas, used nothing but personal vehicles and the Berkeley, California, Police Department required officers to supply their own vehicles for many years. In Newport, Sheriff Donald Ray demonstrated outstanding leadership and initiative with a program of recycling aluminum cans. He wisely recruited the community and involved the citizens. His fund-raising efforts soon resulted in the purchase of four used vehicles and plans for a fifth. Sheriff Ray's insight into the value cost ratio of used vehicles, his lack of hesitation in going to the citizens for help, and his courage to break with tradition, resulted in patrol cars for the police, the desired result. As Sheriff Ray noted, everyone profited. The program helped make the community a cleaner place to live, it provided police cars, and perhaps most importantly it brought the community closer together.

Most larger police departments retire vehicles when they reach a certain mileage accumulation, usually 50,000. Small town and rural police departments frequently operate vehicles with over 100,000 miles on them. Police driven miles depreciate a vehicle faster than normal service so that a police vehicle with 100,000 miles on it appears in the same condition as a vehicle used in normal service for 150,000 miles. Many small town and rural police vehicles are totally worn out. They seem very sick but the police refuse to let them die.

Since small town and rural police can survive with inadequate office facilities less painfully than they can survive with inadequate vehicles, they often find themselves existing rather well in conditions that would prove fatal to big city police departments. All street officers generally consider the car as their office, so the small town or rural officer with literally no office encounters little adjustment.

A surprising number of small town and rural police departments operate without any office. These police departments perform as much office work as possible in the car or in the field. When circumstances demand a more formal office than the close quarters of a car permit, the officer uses an office or conference room in a city or county building. A local cafe or coffee shop may prove more appropriate than the police car. These same police departments rely on other county or city employees for clerical and secretarial support.

A few police departments take special pride in their uniqueness. The Columbia, Mississippi, Police Department consists of fifteen officers housed in a small but neat brick building only twenty-four feet long and eight feet wide. With a bay window on the front, it does somewhat resemble a drive through hamburger stand. However, it is adequate and serviceable and both officers and citizens take pride in their uniqueness.

Periodically, the Carrabelle, Florida, Police Department makes the news with their telephone booth police station. Again, citizens and police enjoy the resulting attention.

A few small town and rural police departments work out of converted restrooms, garages, fire stations, condemned buildings, jails, or heavy equipment barns owned by the county. The convenience, low costs, and

...ality of mobile homes and premanufactured buildings explain ...rapidly growing popularity for city offices and police departments ...mall towns and rural areas.

Aside from the novelty, variation, and adaptability displayed by many small town and rural police departments, the majority of them claim adequate, comfortable buildings and office space. Many enjoy uncrowded, modern, or even new facilities. Minimum office space and facilities seem required to maintain basic police files and correspondence, but modern police communications demands more elaborate investment. Dispatchers should work in a pleasant, distraction-free environment for best results. Too frequently, small town and rural police dispatching jobs expect more than any one person can handle. These situations prove counterproductive and all those associated suffer.

Any more detailed information concerning small town and rural police facilities remains a matter of speculation. Hopefully, I can include accurate estimates of the resources and facilities in the second edition. We need to ascertain if any relationship exists within small town and rural police departments between the adequacy of facilities and the number of officers. I know of police departments with fourteen or fifteen officers working out of deplorable facilities; and police departments with fewer than five officers working in plush, luxurious conditions. Perhaps it will average out; maybe the police departments with ten to fifteen officers enjoy better facilities, or perhaps police departments in the middle with five to ten officers work in the most adequate facilities.

Uniforms, guns, and gunbelts are seldom supplied to officers by small town and rural police departments. A few of these police departments compensate by permitting officers to purchase uniforms from designated common name brand clothing. With all officers on a police department wearing the same colors and styles, these less expensive work clothes serve all the functions of uniforms. Citizens rarely notice any difference. Many small town and rural police departments and sheriffs' offices used khaki work clothes for uniforms for so many years that they still appear in a few agencies as regulation uniforms. My visits with small town and rural police departments in different states also reveal trend setting in head gear. An increasing number permit baseball caps. Small town and rural police departments always tolerate more hatless officers than do larger police departments. Baseball caps with a flash or shield seem to strike a happy compromise between the impractical and nothing.

A recent innovation, one write report writing proves a boon for small town and rural police. The one write system includes standardized forms and requires the officer to write the report only once. The first draft the officer completes in the field is the finished product. This saves typing and time expended in rewriting.

Small town and rural police seem to serve as trendsetters and path finders in terms of handguns. For numerous reasons these police departments appear to be changing from revolvers to semiautomatics at a faster rate than big city police departments. Contrary to their conservative reputation for seldom changing and never trailblazing, they seem to adopt new sidearms faster than other police. Perhaps this change results from a younger average age of the chiefs, a greater percentage of patrol-oriented chiefs, or the lower costs involved in an entire police department switching. Although small town and rural police possess fewer firearm qualification requirements, future surveys may reveal they practice more and seem more skilled in use of firearms. Very limited preliminary observations certainly indicate this. Practice opportunities seem more accessible and frequent.

Volunteer police reserve programs and the can-do attitude of the small town philosophy seem the major salvation of many small town and rural police departments with otherwise marginal resources and facilities.

Police departments of various sizes learn the numerous benefits of a police reserve unit. Police reservists usually include members from every segment of the community volunteering their time to serve the community by helping the police department. The benefits seem many and powerful. Reservists help civilianize policing and demilitarize it. They help the community see and understand that police act as public servants, not as cold uncaring robots. Police reserves donate thousands of hours each year to police efforts in the U.S. Wise chiefs do not ignore or waste such a valuable resource.

With an absolutely minimum investment of planning, coordination, screening, background checks, interviews, and training, any police department can capitalize on this wealth of volunteers. No other option offers a greater return on the investment. Fears that reserve officers include power-hungry psychopaths seem completely unfounded. Proper screening eliminates the few of these that do exist. The vast majority of police reservists include everyday, garden variety people who want to serve their community and feel comfortable in or enjoy the police environment. They sincerely want to serve their community, but they tend to avoid the more traditional methods, such as service clubs and fraternities.

Depending on state law, reservists perform assorted tasks and duties. They gladly do the boring or undesireable police jobs, freeing regular officers for other duties. Even when unarmed they can be depended upon to serve the community in a myriad of ways. They constitute a gold mine in every community. Tradition remains the only explanation as to why more police departments do not take advantage of reserve programs.

Reserve programs can greatly enhance large city police departments, but they can completely change and energize small town and rural police departments. Wise small town and rural chiefs realize the enormous value of tapping this resource. Chiefs may seem suspicious of money from state or federal governments carrying too many strings, but they can easily see that local people have no outside ties. All of their strings lead back to the community. Alert chiefs soon realize that they share a common goal with reservists, better policing.

The can-do attitude of the small town philosophy contributes significantly to effective policing in spite of the adversity caused by inadequate resources and facilities. Small town and rural officers make personal contributions of time, money, and property; and they sacrifice hopes of a better lifestyle promised by employment with a larger police department.

The personal involvement frequently found on small town and rural police departments does not end when the shift is over or because of inadequate salary, resources, or facilities. The individual officer cares about people in the community to such a degree that it generates a police loyalty not found on larger police departments. Small town and rural officers work more hours without compensation than other officers do. Budgets do not always allow overtime, and compensatory time (an equal amount of time the officer does not have to work in compensation for working overtime) proves worthless on many smaller police departments.

In 1974, in the National League of Cities vs. Usery, the U.S. Supreme Court held police departments exempt from minimum wage and overtime laws. Even prior to that, police departments with five or fewer officers were not covered by minimum wage and overtime requirements. Ironically, those police departments needed the protection of the law more than did other police departments. Good faith and fair practices resulted in larger police departments compensating officers properly and fewer incidents of working their officers with no compensation. Organized police labor movements also contribute to this improvement.

However, new legislation will not resolve this problem. The law cannot force people to do the impossible. For example, a serious case develops requiring hours of immediate attention on a small town or rural police department. The budget permits no overtime, so compensatory time remains beyond consideration. The officer coming on duty faces other priority commitments. The officer already involved in handling the case confronts a timeless small town and rural police dilemma: work without pay or add to the mountain of unfinished work and injustice. Police conscience battles economic reality.

Small town and rural officers, because of their police community loyalty, often opt to work and do justice. They volunteer their time to better serve the community. This appears to resolve the dilemma, but instead only shifts responsibility to the chief. The chief now looks downstream and considers the possibility of that officer some day filing a law suit to recoup money owed for forced overtime labor. Many chiefs refuse to assume such risks for the town or county and consequently strictly prohibit officers from working any overtime. Fortunately for the cause of justice, small town and rural police officers continue to work cases on their own time. The chief and town seem relatively safe from a disastrous judgement since the officer clearly violates department policy. Again, justice seems best served when the officer violates department policy.

Small town and rural officers dedicate personal property and even money in much the same way they give their time. A little bit here and a little bit there adds up. Larger police departments supply unlimited batteries for flashlights. Children of these officers never need batteries for Christmas toys. Small town and rural officers must buy their own batteries. Cameras, film, fingerprint powder and brushes, and many other seemingly insignificant items total a significant cost over a period of years. The officer faces yet another dilemma: purchase the items with out-of-pocket money or do without.

Not infrequently citizens come to the rescue of small town and rural police. They donate personal time, money, and property to help improve their police. The volunteer fire department donates labor to help off duty officers refurbish and panel the police station with materials donated by local merchants. No one ever notices the blemishes or factory rejects. In one sense the citizens and police remain indistinguishable. The small town philosophy applies to all in a community, not just one group labeled police. Small town and rural community people suffer together and prosper together.

Insurance in the late 1980s forced an increased number of small towns to suffer. Big towns experience problems; but small towns suffer big problems, problems that remain unthinkable and impossible in bureaucracies. A few big cities carry no insurance but encounter no trouble paying unfavorable judgements out of their huge coffers. Many small towns cannot afford the rising premiums, and they cannot pay small or large settlements out of their dusty coffers.

Only one course of action remains. This situation requires no leadership or decision making. The choice remains inevitable. The town cannot call, or bluff; it must fold. Impossible insurance premiums cause some small towns to disincorporate.

Small towns incorporate in the United States pioneer spirit of remaining independent and autonomous, and sometimes to avoid annexation by a larger city also forcing loss of autonomy. They disincorporate to avoid loss of pride caused by financial disaster. These people possess little more than pride when they incorporate or disincorporate. So even though they lose their police department and other city services at disincorporation, they remain strong and confident as ever in their spirit of small town philosophy. Just as group interaction, not a building, makes a church; group interaction, not a charter, forms a small town or rural community.

Chapter 11

POLICE DEPARTMENTS
WITH FEWER THAN FIVE OFFICERS

EVEN THOUGH small town and rural police are the quintessence of modern policing, those police departments with fewer than five officers possess inherent dilemmas. Their uniqueness does, however, seem limited to considerations within the police department. Characteristics which make small town and rural police unique, such as interaction between officers and citizens, do not vary by size of police department among those police departments claiming fewer than sixteen officers. Police departments employing fewer than five officers that try to operate a full-time operation encounter sizeable problems even with budgets that permit overtime. This topic appears well covered in the Organization and Administration chapter.

To examine one possible problem, police departments with four officers seem in greater danger of a divisive split than other size police departments do. If the chief and one officer continuously act in concert opposing the other two, paralyzing internal strife may result. The balanced numbers of two against two can outweigh the power and influence otherwise inherent in the chief's rank. When this first occurs, it may indicate only a brief oversight by the chief. If it continues, it reflects a weak leader. If allowed to continue, the overall effectiveness of the police department will diminish. The chief likely will suddenly realize a display of favoritism costs the production of two officers, thus resulting in a de facto police department of two.

In such a situation the wise chief would immediately distance himself from the near officer and do everything possible to encourage that officer's joining the other two. A triad of officers remote from the chief remains much preferred over a stalemate of two against two. This enables the chief's rank to regain authority. Even if the lone officer does not join the others, the chief retains more power and position with the singular occupation of the chief's rank. Familarity breeds contempt. Every successful leader understands the dangers of avoiding loneliness of leadership.

On a four-officer police department another triangle, a *triumvirate,* occurs occasionally. The three officers conspire and run the police department. Since a strong leader would never permit such, in most of these cases the chief seems asleep at the wheel, a dullard, or both. My observations indicate that many chiefs who appear asleep at the wheel know full well who leads and controls policing. Many seem lazy and unconcerned, and some enjoy the puppet's role letting others do the work. Just as some officers enjoy drifting aimlessly through forty easy hours each week, so do a few chiefs. In the final analysis, if policing by a triumvirate satisfies the community, criticism seems out of order.

Of the four size police departments discussed here, those with three officers seem ideal. The triangle syndrome works naturally. The chief supervises two persons. Again the chief must avoid any tendency to favor one officer. It remains safer in terms of leadership to find two officers pitted against the chief than one officer and the chief opposing the other officer. Even so, in a police department of three, stalemates cannot exist.

In most of these police departments a natural well-balanced triangle emerges with the chief occupying the upper apex. The two officers must rank the same; otherwise an imbalance creates a rank-heavy, inverted triangle.

Police departments with fewer than four officers must rely on reserves, mutual aid from other police agencies, or a standby on-call system to operate a 24-hour operation. Many police departments with three officers learn from experience what times and what days of the week demand the most police service, and an officer remains on-call at other times.

Many of these small town and rural police departments borrow a communications idea from volunteer firefighters. Each officer maintains a police scanner or receiver at home. This enables officers to assist or cover each other on calls requiring more than a single officer. A well established and trained reserve contingent proves extremely valuable in such situations. Reserves can make the critical difference. They can provide the strength in numbers demanded by safe procedures and police science in certain situations.

Other small town and rural police departments subscribe to a telephone service which permits the dispatcher to ring all the officers at once, and everyone listens to the dispatch on a conference call arrangement.

Police departments with two officers present an excellent test tube study of police partners. Virtually all officers working with a partner soon develop strong bonds which can transcend all else, including discretion, ethics, and even spouses. Officers spend more waking hours with their partners than with their spouses. Crammed into body space violations in a patrol car for eight hours, powerful partnerships evolve to influence policing and change lives. Perhaps more meaningful police philosophy results from these partnerships than from all scholarly efforts combined. The two most fundamental relationships in policing will always remain the human interaction between one officer and one citizen and the bond between police partners.

Group identification seems stronger and more common in small town and rural police departments than it does in other police departments. Just as group identification plays a role in all police partnerships, each officer identifying with a special group of two, it serves an amplified role on police departments with two officers. Although these two may not ride together as partners, special feelings grow from the realization that the individual represents one half of an important community institution. In contrast with police departments of three, where rank seems a necessary visible concern, rank seems never an issue on police departments of two. A police department of two, with the chief apart from the officer, seems the exception; while two-officer police departments with the chief and officer interacting as police partners appear the rule.

Like all police partnerships, individuals on two-officer police departments complement each other. Ignoring rank, officers on these police departments recognize and take advantage of the strengths and weaknesses of each person. Each performs those tasks that experience indicates he can do better than the other.

Synergism contributes to the overall health of these police departments, perhaps even more so than on other small town and rural police departments. Again, the inescapable notion that the individual plays such a magnified role in the community fuels the evolvement of group dynamics. Each of the two seems haunted by a suggestion that he is indispensable. Unlike officers on all other size police departments, each one on a two-officer police department realizes that without him, the group ceases to exist. This distorted sense of importance encourages the development of group dynamics.

In a sense two-officer police departments seem the most basic config-uration, the most pure group. Just as a marriage seems the nucleus of the family which remains the cornerstone of all societies, perhaps the two-officer police department serves as the nucleus of small town and rural police which remain the benchmark of all policing. Like mar-riages, not all two officer police departments result in group dynamics; but a relatively high percentage do, and those provide an ideal labora-tory to study unadulterated policing.

One officer police departments remain anomalies in policing. Tradi-tionally pictured as red-headed, snaggle-toothed stepchildren, they re-main the most maligned, misunderstood, and understudied of all police departments.

Unique in several ways, the image of one person substituting for a major institution seems to explain reluctance in accepting one officer po-lice departments as viable community systems. It seems difficult to clas-sify any one person as a department, institution, or system and impossible to call one a group.

Officers on police departments of two to over 2,000 *represent* the law and their police departments. Each person on a one officer police de-partment *is* the law and the total police department. To many, one offi-cer police departments seem the antithesis of our U.S. police system. In common usage, when employed as a noun, the word police remains plural. Many think of police in plural terms and thus encounter diffi-culty considering police as singular.

When stopped for a traffic violation virtually everyone subcon-sciously feels that this particular officer represents a deviant and does not police like all the others. Comforting rationalization exists in know-ing other officers exist on the same police department. As the lone offi-cer on a one-person police department, this individual seems more intimidating, more unavoidable. No alternative or appeal seems avail-able. We remain most cautious mentally in relinquishing all police powers to any one individual. Outsiders seem tempted to think of the one-officer police department in this manner.

Those more familar with the concept consider the one-officer police department differently. The absence of another officer forces interaction with the community. Police enjoy nothing more than recounting, reliv-ing, and relying with each other their action packed, rolicking adven-tures. Nonpolice types cannot appreciate the fraternal language, humor, and ritual of shared experiences, both real and imagined. Chiefs struggle in vain to break this nonproductive practice and cause the officers to return to work. Individuals on one officer police departments enjoy no choice, they interact with people in the community.

These officers must guard against over policing, or excessive interaction with the same individuals. This lone officer cannot afford to make a nuisance with his mere presence. Without other officers for conversation, this officer should seek out still more individuals in the community and establish more linkages between the police and the community. These officers practice the absolute ultimate in policing. They meet and converse with a wide range of community members on a reoccurring basis in a variety of settings. The tone of this interaction seems always set by the citizen. If the citizen appears in a serious mood and wants to talk serious, the officer complies. In contrast, if the citizen wants humor, friendship, politics, sympathy, gossip, crime, encouragement, a listener, or a talker, the officer accomodates. The officer acts as though this responsibility belongs to the police. The officer satisfies the citizen with police services defined by the community, and makes no attempt to enforce police procedures and tactics as defined and imagined by police.

Caseload and activity vary by the social composition of those policed and the style and philosophy of the police department, not by the size of the police department. The image of the sole police officer in town doing nothing remains a myth. In stark contrast to the big city police department where one officer may hide and do nothing for years, the only officer on a one officer police department cannot escape public scrutiny. Regardless of police workload, citizens quickly notice the absence of the entire police department.

Buford Pusser, the hero of *Walking Tall* fame, though atypical perhaps in his police style and philosophy, did not endure an unusual workload. Being the only officer in a one-officer sheriff's office contributed to his wife's death. She rode along with him to keep him company, as he responded to a bogus call that proved fatal to her. He worked a wide variety of police work, from public service to organized crime. As police chief, constable, and then sheriff, he delivered policing the citizens wanted.

Citizens generally feel a sense of elevated importance when speaking with the police chief as compared to speaking with a patrol officer. In many small towns and rural communities anytime one talks with the police, one talks with the chief.

Of thousands of different size police departments, the single officer police department remains the only size permitting no group dynamics. The one officer police department cannot produce more effects than one person can. The one officer police department stands as one person, nothing more. Undoubtedly police science expects every police department to function as an institution and thus generates an impossible mandate for the one officer police department.

Without the benefit of group dynamics or group identification, this lone officer relies totally on the community for reinforcement and support. Feedback to readjust and fine tune policing comes only from people receiving the services and never from other police. Perhaps future research will suggest that this appears the most effective policing. Perhaps residents of communities policed by one-officer police departments exhibit more influence over their own policing than do people of larger communities. Maybe small towns and rural communities with only a single police officer come closest to perfect self-policing.

Perhaps group dynamics tend to excite some overconfidence and independence. Police departments with two or more officers on occasion delude themselves with ideas they can police without the community's assistance. Since policing remains a reciprocal agreement, these beliefs end in failure. Researchers may find that one officer police departments more frequently understand the necessity of community involvement and police community reciprocity.

Chiefs of big city police departments can gain profound insight into the proper balance of time a chief should spend between administration and public interaction by studying the one officer police department. The chief of the big town police department employs reverse priorities, administration comes first; and, if times remains, then the chief might interact with a few selected citizens. The chief of the one-officer police department interacts and communicates with a cross section of the community; and, if time permits, the chief might engage in limited administration.

The police chief of the one officer police department in Paw Paw, West Virginia illustrates the epitome of this genre. A retired Green Beret, he recruited citizens from the community to help with police duties. Readily confessing that he could not police the town alone, he revealed the key to effective policing. Like gold, genius is where you find it. Profound police thinkers appear on all size police departments, large, small, rural, and smallest. The chief's understanding of community involvement and police community reciprocity will yield valuable dividends for Paw Paw residents. His encouragement for the citizens to police themselves exists as a model to all chiefs and a reminder to all police that one person can make a difference.

Although maligned, ignored, and often ostracised by the rest of the police fraternity, one-officer police departments offer a rare, uncontaminated study of the active ingredient in policing. What they lack in relationships with other officers they compensate with interaction and reciprocity in the community. One officer police departments provide a clear example of how police can totally immerse themselves in the community and completely isolate themselves from stereotypes as distant, aloof, business-like, or above the community. They remind all police of the forgotten importance of customer satisfaction via delivery of police services that people want and expect. One officer police departments remind all police, but especially street officers, of the first commandment of policing: citizens, not the police, define the police role.

One officer police departments can fight crime or enforce the law as well as or better than any other size police department, as Buford Pusser proved. But the vast majority of policing, whether in Los Angeles, California or Paw Paw, West Virginia, does not involve fighting crime or trying to force people to do something they refuse to do; the overwhelming majority of policing involves trying to help people, interacting with people through interpersonal communication, and giving people the impression that the police care. Small town and rural police departments with one officer give the impression they care.

The debate over consolidation of small town and rural police departments crested in the 1970s. Forced to the forefront by the National Advisory Commission on Criminal Justice Standards and Goals recommendation that all police departments with ten or fewer officers consolidate with nearby police departments, the issue generated numerous articles and heated discussions.

The works and findings of Elinor Ostrom, Roger B. Parks, and Gordon P. Whitaker, all of Indiana University, served to permanently extinguish the flames of thoughts favoring consolidation of small town and rural police departments.

Major arguments for consolidation include improved delivery of police services, increased efficiency and effectiveness, and elimination of duplication of services. Little empirical evidence exists supporting any of these positions. Ostrom, Parks, and Whitaker produced significant empirical evidence suggesting the opposite. For example, ten small town and rural police departments with a total of 100 officers requires 10 to 20 percent, or ten to twenty officers, for administration. Consolidating those ten police departments creates a bureaucracy of one hundred which requires about 40 to 50 percent, or officers, to manage the bureaucracy.

Patrol density drops. Consolidation means fewer officers will patrol the streets relative to the population. This in turn means the relative cost of patrol rises. Consolidation clearly decreases efficiency. Small town and rural police remain better able to turn officers on the payroll into officers on the street policing.

No significant studies demonstrate any evidence of duplication of police services by different police departments. Even large police departments farm out certain work to others. For instance, state criminalists may assist a large or small police department with a particular case where their expertise seems required. Police departments tend to complement each other, not overlap. State drug enforcement officers seldom receive anything but a warm reception in small or large towns.

Consolidation results in the loss of personalized service. Under such an arrangement officers from one town frequently respond to police calls in another town. Citizens appear policed by outsiders; something most citizens fear and do not trust. A cornerstone principle of democracy remains local control of police. This seems lost in consolidation.

Administrators choose sides on the consolidation issue based on selfish considerations of future power. Chiefs and sheriffs who stand to gain power from consolidation strongly support it, while executive officers standing to lose power bitterly oppose consolidation.

Again, community satisfaction remains the only valid, reliable measure of police effectiveness. No one bothers to ask the people what they think of police consolidation. Customer satisfaction surveys do not exist in the delivery of police services.

In terms of small town and rural police departments, consolidation remains today nothing more than an impulsive, half-baked idea to make small town and rural police departments look more like bureaucracies. Consolidation does provide greater promise for two or more relatively small bureaucratic police departments wanting to grow and expand the power base. Consolidation seems not to contain a thread of hope for improving policing. Consolidation remains a bureaucratic principle to improve a bureaucracy. Consolidation will not substitute for improved policing.

Chapter 12

CRIME PREVENTION

A STUDY OF small town and rural police aids understanding the nature of crime prevention. Many popular but ineffective programs distort the public's comprehension of preventing crime.

Numerous big city police departments establish elaborate crime prevention programs which do nothing more than promote glossy public relations programs, waste huge amounts of money, and misuse valuable police time. They do not prevent crime. Possibly these crime prevention programs would prevent more crime if the money shoveled into them were taken instead and doled out to street people. Crime prevention programs of big city police departments serve as excellent reminders of the *de facto* purpose of a police bureaucracy. Their goal remains only to perpetuate and reassert the importance of their own existence. Crime prevention efforts give big city police departments a splendid opportunity to persuade citizens of the horrors and fears of crime and criminals and the absolute necessity of maintaining a powerful police force.

Crime prevention remains something citizens, not police, do. When police act like police, ride around on patrol, take reports, enforce the law, and interrogate suspicious persons, they prevent no crime. When police act like citizens and community members, get out of their cars, talk with people, listen to people, and socially interact with all different types of people, they prevent crime.

The startling success of neighborhood watch programs and crimestoppers programs seems easily explained. These programs succeeded because they involved people policing themselves. They required people to participate in the policing process, and they allowed the community members to establish police roles and goals. Who initiates these programs matters little. Getting people involved in the affairs that affect their daily lives seems sure to influence those affairs.

Punishing officers by making them trudge door to door with a canned spiel handing out shiny multicolored phamplets which no one ever reads seems counterproductive at best. One western big city police department gave away thousands of crime prevention booklets which advised among other things, filling hollow core doors with cement. The epitome of cleverly disguised bureaucrats trying to police, I could not contain my laughter when I read one of those booklets. Fortunately, very few police and fewer citizens read them.

Too many crime prevention programs lose sight of their goals in the mechanics of statistics: the length of the tongue of a dead bolt lock (only a kinky police officer could possibly appreciate that anyway) or loudly announcing to the maximum number of people the dates and duration of vacations. Scare tactics sell locks, burglar bars, and insurance, but they do not prevent crime. Small wonder the insurance industry wholeheartedly endorses crime prevention programs.

Small town and rural police critics seem quick to cite the apparent low crime rates as insignificant since so few people live in these jurisdictions. When pressed for explanations, they recite shallow reasons usually involving coincidence or errors in reporting or measuring crime. Very carefully they avoid any hint that citizens and police might play some role in lower crime rates.

Small town and rural communities probably enjoy lower crime rates because of social interaction among group members, strong personal ties between the community and the police, the presence of community-based policing, and the fact that all community members, including the police, hold a vested interest in promoting public safety. The interaction between individual citizens, between individual citizens and individual officers, between individual officers, and between the community and the police department contribute significantly to preventing crime. No possible communication channel remains unused or unimproved in small towns and rural communities.

Big city police departments implement crime prevention programs as a result of crime. They limit themselves by thinking in reactive terms. Small towns and rural communities prevent crime before it happens. No one can ever say how much crime they prevent; no one can measure what did not happen. Speculation does not replace measurement.

Small town and rural communities bask in lower crime rates only because they prevent crime the old-fashioned way; they work together, long and hard. Crime prevention does not happen overnight. Criminals succeed when they work together, long and hard. Citizens of small towns and rural communities understand that nothing less will insure community security.

U.S. firefighters realized decades ago that the best fire-fighting technique remains fire prevention. They immediately busied themselves and involved the public. Every fire department and every firefighter adopted a philosophy of fire prevention. They put in hard work to put themselves out of hard work. As early as the late forties firefighters in small and large towns went into classrooms, even primary grades, businesses, factories, and job sites preaching fire prevention. They experienced great success in selling their product because they genuinely believed in what they taught, fire prevention. They did not talk down to people. They did not sell fire extinguishers or insurance. They sold an attitude, a philosophy, the best way to prevent fires. Buying a fire extinguisher to prevent fires seems the same as buying a pistol to prevent burglary. When a home protection gun kills someone, the chance the dead person will be a friend, relative, or loved one remains forty-five times greater than the chance of that person being an intruder. Firefighters talk fire prevention off duty. They believe it. A few even manage to get enthusiastic about it.

Thinking police also realized decades ago that crime prevention held the only answer to the crime problem, but big city police departments seem unable or unwilling to adopt a new philosophy or indoctrinate newcomers. Stubbornly determined to do the job by themselves, they insist on chasing crooks, arresting people who smoke untaxed homemade cigarettes, and, in the best J. Edgar Hoover tradition, wallowing in perverted fantasy in tons of meaningless statistics.

Small town and rural police evolved along a different branch. Their course more closely resembles that of Japanese police. The Japanese enjoy some of the world's lowest crime rates while enduring some of the world's highest population densities, thus destroying claims by big city police departments in the U.S. that population density explains crime rate variations. While adopting the best in communications and transistorized portable radios, the Japanese police remained in the community in close contact with grass roots people. They successfully managed avoiding the plague of the patrol car. Their police employ numerous devices that require officers going door to door and learning names and faces of residents. This forces officers to stay in touch with the people living in the community. It also produces census data.

In our big cities strangers earn extra money by going into neighborhoods, taking the census, and never returning, while the police watch from air conditioned cars. In our small towns police feel obligated to learn the community and know its people. In small town and rural communities the police includes the community, and the community includes the police.

A strong correlation seems to exist between police providing services to the public that they want and request and lower crime rates. Small town and rural police provide a high level of public service. They respond to every cat in the tree call, lonely widow prowler call, and every stuck car horn call with the same urgency. They graciously accept the idea without question that policing remains nothing more than talking with people. They police with the belief that they should do what the people expect to see police doing. Strange as it may seem, once police sincerely adopt and practice this philosophy, crime rates drop. Someone prevented crime and no one knows who to blame.

Many versions of the same police war-story exist, but they all illustrate the same theme. A mentally ill person called police and complained of invisible little people lighting candles on her front steps and thereby blocking her exit. The responding officer shooed away the invisible trespassers, then swept away the candles with an invisible broom — another satisfied customer. Another version relates how the dispatcher carefully recorded all the information for the bureaucracy, then informed the complainant that invisible police officers were enroute in invisible cars. Weeks later on a repeat call, the dispatcher informed the caller that the invisible officer was backed up with other calls and the caller must wait a long time for service, but to be patient, the invisible officer would not neglect any assignments. While the police laughed, the complainant felt reassurance knowing that others possessed similar problems and confidence in the police knowing that they would help. The police did what the public asked.

Traveling through a small town in North Mississippi, I visited the local constabulary. Upon leaving, I discovered my car keys visible inside my locked car. Three people — the police chief, one officer, and a babbling drunk — tried unsuccessfully to coat hanger burglarize my car. Hollering across the street, they summoned a mechanic who quickly gained entry with a metal cheater. Such service would make anyone feel good about the police.

Small town and rural police seem involved in a partnership with their communities that appears correlated to a reduced crime rate. All people who live and work in small towns and rural communities seem engaged in activities and habits not commonly found in higher crime rate areas. Small town and rural police demonstrate interaction with the community and employ community-based policing. These also seem correlated to lower crime rates. Police providing a high level of public service seem associated with communities experiencing a low level of criminal service. Until contradictory evidence indicates otherwise, it seems safe to conclude that small town and rural police effectively prevent crime as they effectively police. They prevent crime by continuous, sincere, personal interaction with all members of the community. Responding to every call and utilizing every possible opportunity to talk with people serve as a vehicle for interacting. Small town and rural police seem to understand better than others that fulfilling the public's perception of the police remains the only perception that matters and the only way to prevent crime.

Chapter 13

CRIMINAL INVESTIGATION

CRIMINAL investigation includes *crime scene processing, neighborhood canvas, file searches, follow-up,* and *informants.* Employing one or more of these five concepts has proven successful in solving the majority of cases cleared by identifying a suspect or suspects.

Some investigations utilize all five while others use only one. Some investigators depend more on one or two of the five. Their experience causes them to favor certain techniques and methods. Some police departments favor certain methods or remain convinced that some approaches seldom produce results. Not one of the five appears more effective than any of the others. Some of the methods logically will clear more cases given certain circumstances. However, criminal investigators who consistently clear and close a high proportion of their cases ignore none of the five.

Some explanation of terms will assist understanding of how small town and rural police investigate and solve crimes and how their procedures differ from those used by criminal investigators working on big city police departments.

Not all crime comes to police attention. Estimates concerning the amount of unreported crime vary, but it seems reasonable to assume as much as one-half of all crime remains unreported. Reporting rates vary by offense, region of the country, and chemistry of the community.

Some populations tend not to report thefts, or thefts below an approximate value. Other communities shy away from reporting certain types of crime. Rape seems the most underreported crime nationwide. Possibly some correlation exists between reporting rates and victim's confidence in their local police. If a victim or witness perceives that more harm than good will result from calling the police, then that person may not inform the police about a crime. In such situations efforts should concentrate on changing the cause of that perception, not merely changing the perception.

Large city police departments tend to assume the position that they cannot, or will not, do anything about the offense if citizens do not report it. This position remains not without some merit. Many unreported crimes exist completely beyond the long arm of the law. However, lumping all unreported crime in the same forgotten file, as big city police departments frequently do, seems a mistake. Proactive policing reveals many unreported offenses.

Proactive officers detect a great number of otherwise unreported crime. Proactive officers, going much more than half way to meet citizens, receive countless reports from people with a telephone within easy reach, plastered with glow-in-the-dark large police and emergency numbers. Many citizens refuse to call the police and make a report but will gladly explain all the insignificant details to the friendly officer stopping by. Experience indicates that changing the police to seek out and converse with people remains far easier than changing people so they will call police. It seems also much more practical. We know many methods that will cause the officer to approach people. All attempts to change citizens so they will call police fail.

Some crime remains unreported, but police can detect a portion of unreported crime by adopting a proactive philosophy. Of all crime coming to police attention, the portion never solved seems to vary by type of offense, police department, and police department size.

Complicating matters, the majority of police departments do not contribute data to the FBI for inclusion in their annual *Uniform Crime Reports*. Fortunately, big city police departments submit their statistics in a regular fashion so that the vast majority of big city residents, and thus the majority of the United States population, seem fairly represented. Small town and rural police departments remain recalcitrant regarding sending crime data to the FBI, and therefore they and the people they serve do not appear fairly represented in the annual crime reports.

Of those police departments submitting data, a lesser number intentionally distort information for self-serving reasons. This further discredits already notoriously unreliable and invalid annual summaries.

A number of scholarly studies exist regarding small town and especially rural crime; but virtually nothing is known about solution rates of small town and rural criminal investigators, on a nationwide basis. Rural crime appears increasing at a greater rate than does urban crime. Vandalism, theft, and robbery increased 514 percent in nonurban areas in twenty years, according to one report. Other studies suggest property crimes seem high and crimes against the person seem low in small town and rural areas when compared to big city rates.

Generalizing from the very limited small town and rural data in the *Uniform Crime Reports,* one might conclude that a negative correlation exists between population of policed area and percentages of crime cleared by arrest (see Appendix D). It appears that the percentage of documented crimes cleared decreases as police department size increases. Such generalizing entails dangerous assumptions. This conclusion assumes communities of similar populations maintain police departments of similar sizes, an assumption clearly at odds with reality, and previously discussed.

Ignorance far exceeds knowledge concerning small town and rural crime rates and attendant solution rates. Efforts to separate crime rates, victimization rates, crime causation, clearance rates, policing styles and philosophies, and the social nature of communities, perhaps attempt the impossible. Each of these variables may interact to varying degrees with the others. Predicting one may depend on awareness of the others. Future multiple variant analysis will prove intriguing.

The criminal investigator who continually encounters success ignores none of the five methods of solving crimes because all five represent information sources. Of countless available information resources, experience proves these five the most fruitful in criminal investigation. The best criminal investigators remain alert for little known or unusual sources of information that may solve a particular crime.

Criminal investigators deal in information; data remain their life and body and soul — without it they wither and fade away; while with it they solve crimes. The more data sources an investigator uses, the more crimes he will close. Effective investigators work in volume and probabilities. Criminal investigators working with big city police departments virtually always must work with unreasonable time constraints resulting from impossible case loads and uncaring bureaucracies.

Effective investigators process greater amounts of data on the chance of identifying a lead. When time permits they process more data regardless of lesser chances, in hopes of finding a long-shot lead. When all data in a case appears processed and bleached clean, the criminal investigator begins eliminating leads. Investigators expand a case by collecting data and identifying leads until the data base seems exhausted. Then investigators narrow the focus of the case by eliminating leads and false suspects. In cases where the resources, leads, suspects, and time appear exhausted or eliminated, investigators must move on to other cases. In many cases a lack of time and nothing else causes the investigator to abandon it.

Crime scene processing involves searching the crime scene and immediate surrounding area for sources of information, people, and evidence. It involves locating, identifying, documenting, recording, collecting, preserving, and marking evidence.

Small town and rural police probably invest more time and less money in crime scene processing than do big city police departments. Evidence easily overlooked might remain undiscovered by the investigator in the big city but located by the small town or rural criminal investigator. Evidence requiring expensive, sophisticated local equipment would more likely prove valuable to the criminal investigator employed by a larger police department.

The increasing availability of crime lab facilities aids all criminal investigators. However, portable vacuum cleaners, glass vials, plaster casting materials, small video cameras, and other tools that make the job easier are found with greater frequency on the larger police departments.

Among small town and rural police departments a rather clear distinction possibly emerges between those employing fewer than seven or eight officers and those with nine or ten to fifteen officers. Police departments with fewer than seven or eight officers seem to possess fewer technical tools and less hardware to assist criminal investigators than does the other group of police departments. Future studies may find that all police departments with more than seven or eight officers tend to maintain more tangible criminal investigative resources. Perhaps two or more distinctions occur and not merely one.

Following the conviction of a serial murderer in Atlanta, Georgia, in 1982, crime scene processing places greater emphasis on the value of physical evidence. Trace evidence, dust, dirt, hair, fibers, lint, and microscopic particles play a greater role in criminal investigation and gaining convictions. Securing witnesses at crime scenes and testimony remain important or even crucial to criminal investigation. However, criminalistics demand and deserve more attention in modern criminal investigation. A few brave criminal investigation thinkers now advocate that in a forced choice situation, between securing witnesses or physical evidence, the investigator should secure the physical evidence.

Neighborhood canvassing solves crime. It involves the investigator searching for witnesses or persons who might contribute any information about the crime. It extends far beyond the immediate crime scene to the limits of the investigator's imagination. A minimum neighborhood canvass checks each potential information source along avenues of approach and escape.

Neighborhood canvassing must include every location where people exist for it to produce data and leads. Neighborhood canvassing includes factories, businesses, streets, highways, street people, residences, fire towers, gas stations, coffee shops, etc. Neighborhood canvassing seems like an Easter egg hunt. The criminal investigator assumes the information exists; finding it remains the challenge. Crimes without clues detectable in scientific neighborhood canvassing appear rare as Easter egg hunts with no hidden eggs.

Anniversary observations fall somewhere between crime scene processing and neighborhood canvassing. Investigators reviewing the crime scene twenty-four hours or one week later, or the same date of the next month, may identify people with valuable leads whose habits or routines carry them through or near the crime scene area on a predictable schedule. Road blocks established on crime anniversaries often reveal route drivers, shift workers, commuters, suspects, and others with information related to the crime which would remain unknown without the anniversary observation.

Small town and rural criminal investigators realize greater benefit than do investigators with big city police departments from crime anniversary experiences since these practices require time, not money.

Criminal investigators repeatedly successful in neighborhood canvassing employ polished interviewing techniques. They do not ask questions easily answered with yes or no, such as, "Did you see anything suspicious?" Even if the person does possess valuable information, the officer provides them an easy out. Like a good door-to-door sales representative, the producing canvasser knows that trust and confidence precede giving information. Human nature dictates that most people do not buy from or give information freely to those they do not trust. Contrary to popular opinion, the police uniform or badge in a leather case does not establish trust; otherwise some sales reps would don uniforms and identification in a diamond studded gold case.

Since neighborhood canvassing involves more time than money, small town and rural criminal investigators more frequently than their counterparts on large police departments make greater use of this valuable crime solving method. Small town and rural investigators also profit more from the advantage of closer ties with the neighborhoods they canvass. Frequently, at least a part of the necessary trust seems already established.

Again, great difficulty appears with attempts to separate neighborhood canvassing from police community relations. A police department

that goes the extra mile to serve well seldom encounters completely fruit-
less neighborhood canvasses. The police department putting nothing
into a neighborhood can expect repayment in kind come canvassing
time. Perhaps this explains why so many big city police departments do
not even bother trying to gather information through such means; they
know what will result.

File searches, like crime scene processing and neighborhood canvasses, solve crime. Although wise detectives successfully used files
years ago, the advent of computers expanded the potential of the
criminal investigator to previously unimagined capabilities. An increasing number of police departments now maintain computers. Although
many police departments use computers only for record retrieval, some
experiment with data base programming and invariably are rewarded
by identifying more suspects and putting more criminals behind bars.

The speed with which computers can scan a sea of information permits the criminal investigator to do things in seconds that proved impossible years ago. Doing their best, larger police departments in years past
maintained dozens of different files. Each file contained all the entries of
one field, such as names, arrests, addresses, modus operandi, nick-
names, case numbers, dates, types of crime, or locations. Thus, the
number of files the police department maintained limited the investigator primarily to those leads. Hand purging the records on the probability of finding one entry without a file heading remains today impossible.

For example, if the investigator developed a lead consisting of a nickname, then he could quickly identify all persons using that name if the
agency maintained a nickname file. However, if the lead involved a
height, missing finger, tattoo, or red striped jacket, the investigator remained stymied and frustrated because this information was not in-
dexed by file prior to the computer. Extreme frustration arose from a
detective knowing the needed information existed in the files but remained unretrievable. No files existed for those fields, eventhough the
records contained the entries. Now appropriately programmed computers inform the investigator within seconds of all persons of a certain
height, missing a finger, tattooed with a particular design, or associated
with a red striped jacket. The Easter eggs existed all the time, just hidden in places impossible to reach.

As if to show off, a computer can also rank order or assign values to
records by calculating probabilities. Only police imagination limits
neighborhood canvassing and, given a computer, file searches now seem
limited only by police imagination.

Computers with their bells, whistles, lights, and software cost too much for most small town and rural police departments. Initial costs and expenses mean computer systems with criminal investigation programs appear with much greater frequency on larger police departments. This results in big city police departments benefiting the most, enjoying improved closure rates, and generally solving more crime, thanks to computers.

Even prior to computers, criminal investigators on big city police departments realized greater benefits from file searches than did their counterparts on small town and rural police departments. Big city police departments maintained more current, elaborate files than did small towns or rural communities. Some small town and rural police departments see no need for files, much less computers. A few police administrators, so narrow-minded a fly could straddle their nose and scratch out both eyes, rejoice in reciting a few individual experiences which prove to any village idiot why files seem unnecessary. "It was good enough for yesterday, it's good enough for tomorrow."

Small town and rural criminal investigation efforts that cripple along with limited or no files fall further and further behind. Today, small town and rural police departments without files deny reality. Tomorrow, police departments without computer-assisted criminal investigation will cause their communities to suffer needless victimization.

Computers improve the quality of life. They revolutionize many occupations, including criminal investigation. In the next few years computers will aid criminal investigation in breaking free of the shackles and chains of tradition and cause it to begin realizing its full potential. For small town and rural police to continue delivering quality police services, of which criminal investigation remains a major part, they must adopt and adapt to computers.

Future criminal investigators can use computers or guard vacant lots and corn fields. No other choices exist. A strong correlation appears to be emerging between police departments augmenting criminal investigation with computers and police departments enjoying unprecedented clearance and closure rates. These results produced by the marriage of computers and criminal investigation do not discriminate on the basis of police department size. Predictably, as the word spreads of the success of big city police departments using computers, small town and rural citizens will gradually grow to expect the same. How these expectations will cohabitate with the traditional lack of funds appears unknown.

Follow-up in criminal investigation consists of recontacting the victim, witnesses, and all other persons involved to collect and record any new developments or leads. As a last resort, recontact with all suspects might prove worthwhile. Experience indicates that follow-ups solve crimes. Like neighborhood canvassing, follow-ups seem more productive when undertaken by someone with good interviewing skills.

The strength of follow-ups lies in part with latent police detective curiosity residing in almost everyone. Victims and witnesses contemplate, worry, speculate, gossip, relive, rethink, reconsider, and develop good suspects and leads with astonishing accuracy. They also develop millions of worthless leads, but good criminal investigators work in volume and probabilities.

Since up to eighty percent of interpersonal communications remains nonverbal, follow-ups seem most effective when accomplished in the field. Telephone follow ups appear little more effective than no follow-ups.

All follow-ups serve a powerful police community relations role. Recontacts that produce no leads still build and reinforce peoples' trust and confidence in the police. The citizen perceives the police as working hard on their individual case and caring about them as a human. Fortunately for the police, very few citizens ever learn just how little the police do in the average case. Perception seems more important than reality. Therefore, criminal investigators can fight frustration with the knowledge that totally nonproductive follow-ups do not exist; they exist in perception, but not in reality.

Follow-ups require greater time and lesser or no money. Criminal investigators on large police departments who follow-up active cases usually cannot afford the necessary time locating people in the field. They rely almost exclusively on the telephone for follow-up work. Many of these investigators do no follow-ups on nonfelony cases; while others conduct follow-ups only on certain felony cases. Police departments that do not care enough to dispatch an officer to take a felony report probably will not care enough to follow-up on that same case, and consequently the possibility of those police departments solving such crime seems less than outstanding.

Small town and rural criminal investigators generally appear to utilize the follow-up concept. Apparently they do not encounter the difficulties presented in big cities of locating and recontacting people. Greater personal interaction among citizens might also result in a greater percentage of follow-ups producing valid leads. Follow-ups in small towns and rural communities help to strengthen police community ties in addition to solving cases.

Vollmer policing demands follow-up on all unresolved criminal cases and many noncriminal cases. Follow-up remains a vital part of criminal investigation, which remains an integral part of policing. Investigating crimes without following-up seems similar to policing without public contact.

When a criminal investigator sees a complex case finally gel only because of an informant, the investigator seems likely to conclude that informants remain unsurpassed as means to solve crime. Using informants seems perhaps the oldest criminal investigative method, and informants will remain forever a rich source of information.

The line between informants and informers remains unclear even among police. Some general agreement exists to define informers as those who give information to the police on a one time only basis and to define informants as those who give information to police on a reoccuring basis. The issue seems unworthy of lengthy discussion since both groups possess useful information. Effective criminal investigators depend on both groups and never overlook the possibility of an informer evolving into an informant. Contrary to popular opinion, most informants do not receive money for the information they supply.

Access to information about crime and a willingness to share that information with police, make an informant. Since some occupations and vantage points provide increased access to that information, informants seem easily categorized by their position in the community. Bearing in mind that informants may and do occur anywhere, past experience indicates the three most common sources of informants remain well placed individuals, persons on the fringes of crime, and criminals themselves.

Well placed individuals include all persons who meet the public in the course of their jobs. Those positioned to overhear small talk, gossip, and conversation not intended for the informants ears relay superb information. Human nature assumes privacy too frequently. Only the best of criminals never drop their guard. This group of informants includes secretaries and clerks who meet the public, cosmetologists, waiters, busboys, and people who work where groups of people wait, such as airports and bus stations. This group also includes people who do not necessarily meet the public but who remain positioned to gather evidence, such as postal carriers, trash collectors, and persons delivering newspapers. Anyone routinely traversing the neighborhood may potentially serve as extensions of the investigator's eyes and ears.

The second group, persons on the fringe of crime, overlaps the first and includes those persons whose positions seem frequently exposed to criminals. This group includes bartenders, cabbies, and many street people. It also includes anyone whose position places them in frequent or repeated association with criminals. Bartenders alone appear responsible for solving countless crimes.

The last group overlaps with street people and consists of the criminals themselves. Dopers, prostitutes, thieves, con artists, nickle-dime mobsters, has-beens and never-will-bes deal information when it serves their best interests and when they perceive no other acceptable alternatives. This group presents the greatest challenges and rewards. They seem the most challenging because they remain professional liars; they earn a living lying to and deceiving people. Unlike most criminal investigators, the majority of criminals spend every waking hour studying, practicing, and refining their skills and grew up doing that. Like criminal investigators, criminals include the intelligent and shrewd and the proud and successful. They offer the greatest rewards because they exist closest to the heartbeat and action of crime. Their's is a life of crime, and sometimes it takes a thief to catch a thief.

The use of informants appears determined more by the social nature of the community and police department tradition than by police department size. Criminal investigators representing all categories of police department sizes use informants with impressive results. Informants remain probably the oldest and most universal criminal investigation method. Evidence indicates the reliance on informants by investigators will not significantly decrease in the foreseeable future.

Illegal drugs and their ever present family of problems appear in U.S. cities, towns, and communities without regard to size or social nature of the population. However, denial of drug problems seems greater in small towns and rural communities. Criminal investigators in these communities often shock the residents with the first drug case or the first relatively large drug bust.

Street police officers and criminal investigators who know their state laws concerning controlled substances and laws of search and seizure encounter few problems originating drug cases. Proactive officers find dope and make good strong cases with predictable frequency while engaged in nothing more than work-a-day policing.

Street officers who maximize their number of vehicle stops will stumble over more dope than the average citizen knows to exist. All good criminal investigators work in volume. Any police officer who works in volume will work volumes of dope. Dope does not enter the pockets, homes, offices, lunchboxes, toolboxes, and schoolrooms of the United States via molecular particle beaming but via the streets, highways, and vehicles in the U.S. From Telluride to Nome to Tarpon Springs, dope moves on the same roads as police. With the quantity and quality of virtually all drugs increasing, no respite appears soon.

As discussed in a previous chapter, some evidence suggests that patrol officers serve as defacto criminal investigators. That premise seems well supported in the prevalence of originations of drug and narcotic law violations. Even though all fifty states defelonized their marijuana laws, origination of felony marijuana cases by street officers remains so common newspapers generally ignore them.

Small town, and especially rural, police enjoy the added challenge of spotting cultivation violations. They often invest considerable time in surveilance of plots to identify growers and owners but one bingo makes the waiting on a dozen cases worthwhile.

Small town and rural police, like virtually all police, restrict themselves in dope cases with a dope on the table mentality. Absolutely obsessed with quantifiable seizures, kilos, pounds, tons, lids, plants, joints, and bales, they bury their head in the sand and pretend that big time dope movers and organizers do not exist. Most police seize dope as if it remained a dwindling supply of a nonrenewable resource.

Many big time drug traffickers appear most knowledgeable about varying drug enforcement priorities by size of police department and even by state. They hire the best lawyers that money can buy and possess the wisdom of experience. Like good criminal investigators, they work in volume and probabilities. Many reside in small towns and rural areas since they believe doing so improves chances of avoiding detection.

Small town and rural police can learn and develop indicators and profiles to aid in spotting drug runners. Then, with probable cause for another violation, officers can stop vehicles and investigate. Small town and rural police should know all the airports and unpaved runways in their jurisdictions. They must work closely with prosecutors and magistrates in developing plans for handling drug cases.

Developing a plan, deciding how to best approach a particular situation, or what to put in a report and what to omit, must happen before a case surfaces, if success remains the goal. Bruce Olson, a former Berkeley, California, police officer developed and published an outstanding package on report writing for police trainers to use. The package seems so complete with detail that it appears especially appropriate for small town and rural police departments.

Precisely how much drug trafficking happens in small town and rural U.S. remains unknown. The drug-free community exists today only as an endangered species. In virtually all small towns and rural areas the officer or criminal investigator wanting to work drug cases remains unlimited by a lack of offenses. Small town and rural police administrators and civic leaders who encourage police to look the other way and not risk damaging fragile reputations accomplish more harm than good. They undermine the future health and integrity of their own social environment.

Organized crime does not exist without some degree of local corruption. Just as towns, cities, and communities receive the policing they demand, so they coexist with the amount of organized crime they are willing to tolerate. Communities not objecting to vice or organized crime virtually always enjoy the benefits, and pay the price, of this social cancer. In contrast, those communities who refuse to permit organized crime or vice to leech from their people seldom exhibit any evidence of either. Organized crime knows too many hospitable locations to waste resources fighting their hosts. Like most noncriminal types, organized criminals do not relish living where they appear unwanted.

The relative presence of organized crime and vice seems determined more by the social composition and tolerances of the community, police and prosecution pressures, and tradition, than by the size of the police department.

Small town and rural police given the green light to combat vice or organized crime will succeed in inverse proportion to the extent of the cancer. If the small town or rural community appears free of any symptoms, or exhibits only a few fresh indicators, the police department will possibly experience little difficulty in removing the advanced party and maintaining a town with no organized crime. If the small town or rural community suffers advanced symptoms, the small town or rural police department remains helpless in achieving any measureable success.

Organized crime remains a highly successful and profitable enterprise because, like all successful organizations, it organizes; and, like many, it organizes on a nationwide and international basis. The premium grade cocaine snorted by high school seniors in small towns of the

U.S. does not originate locally. Small town and rural police remain unorganized as a group at state and national levels. They also lack the sophistication, resources, and tactical and strategic intelligence to effectively remove even part of the disease.

However, small town and rural police seem compensated with an indomitable spirit. They sometimes do the impossible. Small town and rural Sheriff Bufford Pusser sent organized crime gangsters to prison. The more cynical suggest that signed his death warrant. Several other examples exist scattered throughout the U.S. of small town or rural criminal investigators appearing to strike a significant blow for justice against organized crime. Perhaps these incidents appear too infrequently to represent anything more than anomalies.

Of all personal characteristics of successful criminal investigators, none serves better than persistence. Johnny Bonds, the cop who wouldn't quit, remains an inspiration to all criminal investigators. Fighting impossible odds and unrelenting discouragement, he perservered. His lonely but determined efforts resulted in reclassifying two suicides as murders and identifying, locating, arresting, and assisting in the conviction of a mass murderer. His personal sacrifice remained great, the case cost him his wife and family, but justice was done because of his hard work, criminal investigation, and determination.

Dr. James Gilbert, a former Berkeley, California, police officer, wrote *Criminal Investigation,* a widely used college textbook and a superb introduction to the subject.

In summary it appears those criminal investigation methods and techniques requiring a greater investment of time and a lesser investment of money seem favored and emphasized by small town and rural investigators. Limited again by fiscal resources, small town and rural criminal investigators improvise, adapt, and learn to do without.

The lesson here for police science remains how much criminal investigators can do with so little. Interpersonal relationships and communication between the citizenry and the police department undoubtably play a major role in clearance and closure rates. As criminal investigators in larger cities increase their dependence on computers, crime solution rates will improve, or at worst slow their graveyard spiral. Unable to afford computers, small town and rural police in general can anticipate few improvements in criminal investigation. Any differences in criminal investigation by police department size in the future will seem skewed in favor of the larger police departments because of computers.

Chapter 14

YOUNG PEOPLE AND OLD PEOPLE

POLICE MUST communicate and interact with all age groups if they wish to remain effective. Officers who seem to avoid certain age groups only police a portion of the community. Unfortunately for the image of policing nationwide, some officers focus their attention on middle-aged individuals while prefering to minimize contact with the young and old. Proactive police cannot discriminate on the basis of age.

In another ironic twist of policing, police as a group fail to associate their involvement with youth and the possibility of a future reduction in crime. The fact that police are results-oriented prevents them from giving serious consideration to long range programs. They construct countless police community relations programs in hopes that positive results will soon appear. In shocking contrast, police generally avoid geniune efforts at police juvenile relations programs because positive results require years for fruition.

Officers' typical feelings toward the very young and the very old magnify this irony. The rare expressions of police sympathy seem most often aroused by criminals victimizing the very young or the very old. These two extreme age groups remain the most defenseless and consequently the most likely to elicit tightly held police sympathies. Police avoid these two groups until after the crime, and then police sympathize. These people do not need or want sympathy; they need and want help before the crime.

Small town and rural police departments differ in several ways from big city police departments in the treatment of juveniles. Although small town and rural police departments often keep poorer and fewer records and files than other police departments keep, considerable evidence does exist indicating that small town and rural police departments tend to dispose of a greater percentage of juvenile cases on an informal basis.

Statistics suggest that juveniles taken into custody by small town or rural police seem much more likely candidates for petitions and entry into the formal juvenile justice system than juveniles taken into custody by officers in larger cities. However, taken into custody means taken to the police station. Larger police departments possess more rules and regulations and remain more likely to require officers to bring juveniles to the police department for any disposition. Small town and rural police departments possess fewer rules, less formality, no bureaucratization, and appear less likely to transport juveniles to the police station when the case seems best handled in the community by those involved.

Juveniles transported to the small town or rural police station appear involved in serious cases with greater frequency and thus are more likely to enter the formal juvenile justice system than do juveniles taken to big city police departments. In contrast police juvenile contacts resulting from offenses or complaints in small town and rural communities seem more likely to end in informal adjudication in the field and no trip to the station than do similar contacts in larger cities. Combining these two observations leads to the conclusion that compared to the police of larger cities, small town and rural police dispose of a greater percentage of juvenile cases in the field; but of those juveniles taken to the police station the police refer a greater percentage to the formal juvenile justice system.

It appears reasonable to assume that small town and rural police frequently use liberal discretion in disposing of juvenile cases in the field and police station. Personal relationships seem more likely to influence decisions. Perhaps such informal, personal handling of cases discriminates unjustly against certain groups of young people. Both sides of the issue contain persuasive considerations. Both sides argue for the same goal, helping the juvenile, but disagree on the most appropriate methods.

Small town and rural police rarely include a juvenile specialist. Small town and rural officers remain virtually always generalists. Although the street officer remains the primary juvenile officer, the presence of a specially trained juvenile officer can only serve to improve police juvenile relations and encourage handling serious cases in a more polished and appropriate manner.

The Delinquency Control Institute in Los Angeles, California, remains the finishing school for police officers specializing in juvenile work. The International Juvenile Officers' Association provides benefits and the opportunity to communicate and interact with officers sharing similar concerns and problems.

Dr. John P. Kenney, a former Berkeley, California, police officer served as the primary coauthor of *Police Work With Juveniles and The Administration of Justice.* It remains the definitive study of the subject.

Numerous avenues exist for small town and rural police departments to educate and better train juvenile officers. Frozen inactive by tradition and meager resources, small town and rural police departments seem satisfied with their police juvenile relations.

Improved police juvenile relations for small town and rural police require a shift in attitude and a sincere commitment by the police. They must realize that successful, effective police juvenile relations call for the police going more than half way to join the communities' youth. Youth and police can lose so little and gain so much that difficulty arises in understanding why such great hesitation exists. The conservative, never changing nature of small towns and rural communities remains the only sensible explanation. Boat rockers and wave makers seem unwelcome on all police departments, but they appear to enjoy a slightly better survival rate on the larger ones.

Small town and rural police avoid the elderly in much the same manner as do too many other institutions. Commonly-held perceptions picture the elderly as suffering relatively high victimization rates. Evidence suggests they endure disproportionately higher victimization rates only in the crime of muggings. This leads to speculation that small town and rural elderly may not suffer higher crime rates in any offense.

Fear of crime among the elderly seems much higher than it does in other age groups. Police can strike a blow for police community relations while reducing fear of crime by maximizing contacts with the elderly. The elderly serve as extra eyes and ears in the community for police unafraid to ask. Like juveniles, the elderly can often serve as valuable sources of information for the criminal investigator.

However, to benefit from the potential use of these groups, police must establish a strong two-way relationship. These groups do not remain fertile deposits for the police to occasionally dart in, grab what they need, and rush away. Police must nourish, cultivate, and value their relationships with both these groups for effective policing of the total community.

When the United States begins showing more attention to the old and the young, the police will parrot their communities. Increased attention directed towards older citizens in recent years seems best explained by their increased numbers and ballot power. Young people, forever lacking voter strength, seem destined to remain second class citizens, in the eyes of the public and police.

Chapter 15

THE FUTURE OF SMALL TOWN
AND RURAL POLICE

SMALL TOWN and rural police possess a greater number of desirable characteristics and a lesser number of undesirable characteristics for ideal policing than does any other group of officers. Small town and rural police regularly exhibit those practices, skills, and attitudes associated with effective policing. They continue to model effective policing for others in the police fraternity. This is not a physical model of the mechanics or appearances of policing, but rather a model of the very essence of policing, the personal, social, sincere, helping, informal, involved attitudes and philosophy of people helping people.

Small town and rural police are those officers employed by a police department with fifteen or fewer full-time officers. Whereas bureaucracies determine the quality and effectiveness of police service in larger cities, small town and rural police services result from the phenomena associated with small groups. Where the bureaucracy begins, small group functions end. Small groups and bureaucracies remain mutually exclusive since they pursue opposing goals. Group dynamics, psychological group formation, and reoccuring personal, face-to-face interaction produce effective policing. These small group attributes rarely exist in groups of more than fifteen people.

Other than differences between small groups and bureaucracies, the size and social nature of a community, not the size of the police department, determine the nature of the police.

Reoccuring interaction for nonpolice reasons between small town and rural officers and community members integrates the police and the community in a fashion unknown in larger cities. Bureaucratic

195

principles work to separate the police from the community while small group principles function to blend people and police in an inseparable mixture of self policing.

Since effective policing results from interpersonal communication and social interaction, any attempts to isolate or measure individual independent variables influencing policing seem predestined to fail. But small group principles no longer control graduate schools and think tanks. They acquired excess weight and expanded into bureaucracies, so the search intensifies for that one secret variable or combination to explain all the many differences in the effects of policing. The bureaucracy with a graduate school mentality seeks the nonexistent. A single, previously undiscovered variable to account for greatly improving policing does not exist. However, if it did, it would certainly closely resemble education.

U.S. policing will improve almost immediately after police officers' average educational levels surpass those levels of the general public but not before. Neither bureaucracies nor those with lesser education can police. Armies and soldiers going unprepared into battle will lose and die. Officers with lesser education remain unprepared to police effectively.

The gap between police and citizens in larger cities slowly widens only because the disparity between the educational levels of those two groups increases. Many variables interact to produce police effectiveness in small towns and rural communities. Average police educational levels that equal or exceed those of the citizens contribute to effective policing in small towns and rural communities.

Police officers choosing to work in small towns and rural communities will encounter the exact same advantages, and disadvantages, as experienced by doctors, lawyers, teachers, and ministers electing to spend their careers outside of big cities. Training will not vary significantly from that of their counterparts in the larger cities because of occupational expectations, recommendations, and standards. In comparison to big cities the salaries will be less. Ages of police officers do not vary by size of department, but they may reflect the average age range of the community in small towns and rural areas. Police officers, teachers, nurses, truck drivers, lawyers, and all others living and working in small towns and rural areas enjoy countless benefits available only in such an environment.

Increased public safety, less crime and fear of crime, a totally different lifestyle and atmosphere, different values, traditions, mores, and priorities, a greater sense of belonging to a group and the community, a different and distinct collective personality, and a clearer sense of purpose and direction are only some of the advantages. One does not have to be rich to live in a small town or rural community, but virtually every person residing in a small town or rural area is wealthy by virtue of the surroundings.

Community-based policing resulting from near ideal police community relations remains the forte of small town and rural police. They meld with their communities in a synergistic manner that cultivates and encourages self policing. All community members, including the police, strongly identify with the group and feel a driving need to contribute to that group. Without a bureaucracy to protect them, small town and rural residents enjoy feeding input into the system. They clearly understand that they possess a vested interest in both the process, self policing, and the output, increased public safety.

The many facets of community spirit and small town philosophy form the foundation stones of community-based policing. Small town and rural residents realize that their individual goals and the goals of their community share much in common. Since the individual and the community strive towards the same end, they frequently combine efforts producing synergistic results. When the ends concern public safety then the efforts manifest as self policing resulting in community-based policing.

Machiavelli observed that mercenaries and foreigners do not make good soldiers; they do not have their heart in the cause. The vast majority of officers working in larger cities, and thus the majority of all police, do not live in the community where they police. Instead they live in the suburbs, small towns, and rural communities. Although this says something about their judgement in choosing a homesite, it simultaneously erects insurmountable barriers to effective policing in the larger cities. These *commuter* police claim no vested interest in the outcome of their work. The best and most sincere good faith efforts of leaders in a large police bureaucracy can never overcome the time-clock mercenary logic of commuter police.

In contrast, small town and rural police work where they live. They do have their heart in the cause. These officers do not police strangers, foreigners, or deviants; they police their relatives, families, friends, acquaintances, neighbors, other community (group) members, and even their enemies. They police in a humanistic vein because they police within their own group. They must live with the results of their work.

The small town or rural police officer plays a crucial role because he lives in a community that practices self policing. These officers are group members appointed to help the group police itself. They are insiders working with and helping other community members, not outsiders commuting to a hostile job site to police strangers.

The old adage, "If you want something done right, do it yourself," explains much of the success and effectiveness of small town and rural police. As community members, small town and rural officers police more effectively. They police their own group: fellow community members, each other, they police themselves.

Since the essence of policing remains interpersonal communication and social interaction, skills required for policing include people skills and generalists skills. The absence of specialization on small town and rural police departments actually contributes to increasing police effectiveness. Without special skills the officer must rely on interacting with others. Specialization increases with department size, but it always exists only to support the police officer in the field. Specialization cannot police. Small town and rural police are generalists. They help people in a general way to increase public safety. Being generalists they stay in closer contact with other community members. This leads to stronger ties joining the community and the police which in turn causes more effective policing.

Small town and rural police exhibit greater patrol density and consequently lesser police costs than do the police of larger cities. Patrol density means the ratio of police officers on the street at any given time per 1,000 citizens in the community. As patrol density increases, the costs of policing decrease. The small town or rural citizen receives more police services for his police tax dollar than does his friend living in a larger city.

By combining three common styles of policing with the two major police philosophies and a continuum of police community relations, a typology of policing developed. Demonstrating a proactive philosophy and a service style, small town and rural police emerge as a model of effective policing. More frequently than any other group or classification of police small town and rural police provide the services in the manner that the citizens expect and request. Small town and rural police are able to do this only because they forever remain a part of the community.

During the past twenty years great lip service and knee jerk motion and less reasoned action has been aimed at professionalizing the police. First efforts involved front loading tons of money into police potholes. It was a miserable failure. Money polices no better than do bureaucracies, specialization, strangers, or the undereducated. Second wave attempts at professionalizing the police, fortunately, have resulted in some limited degree of success in a few of the larger police departments. These few officers belonging to the second generation of police professionals now join the small town and rural police genre. This second wave succeeds where interpersonal communications and social interaction between the individual police officer and the individual citizen are enhanced and reinforced.

Unfortunately, no commonly excepted definition of professional police exist today in the United States. Many other countries decided long ago what they wanted from the police. In the United States two paradoxical definitions of professional police exist. One measures police efficiency in absolute, quantifiable, formal, impersonal, objective terms. The other judges police effectiveness by standards that are personal, informal, subjective, qualifiable, and human. As long as bureaucracies like The Police Foundation and The International Association of Chiefs of Police define police, professional police, and policing, small town and rural police will, by those definitions, remain ignored. As long as people receiving police services measure police effectiveness, small town and rural police will model the epitome of everything policing can be.

The future of small town and rural police appears bright because the future will reflect their past. Small town and rural police will continue superb policing.

APPENDIX A
POSSIBLE RELATIONSHIPS

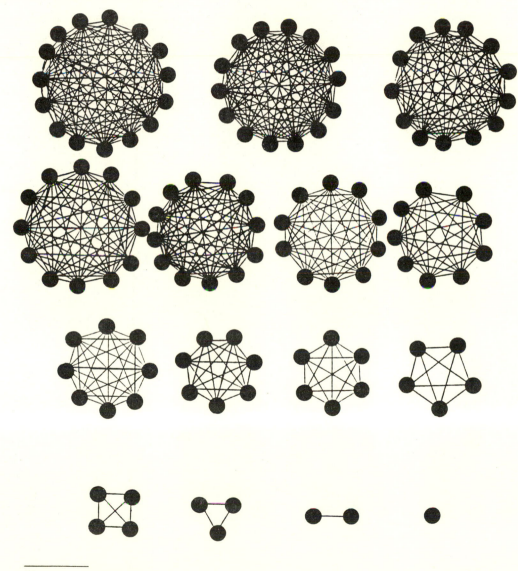

Illustrations by Jim Sims.

APPENDIX B
ORGANIZATION CHARTS

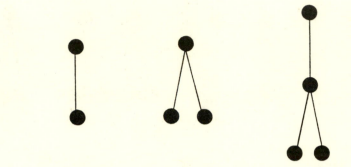

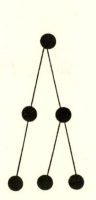
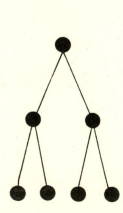

(APPENDIX B CONTINUED)

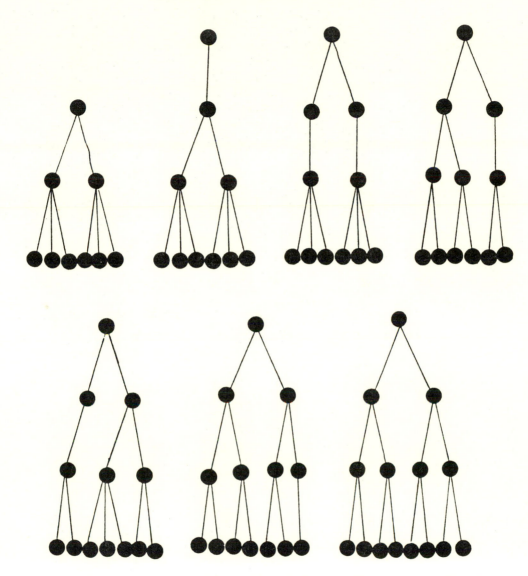

APPENDIX C

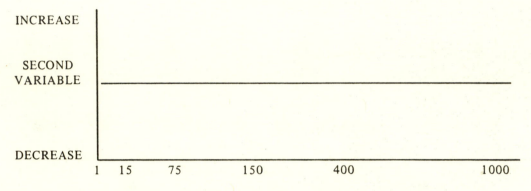

Number of officers employed by a police department.

No correlation exists between the number of officers employed by a police department and:

> *hours of training
> *police tasks
> *officers' ages
> *military experience

APPENDIX D

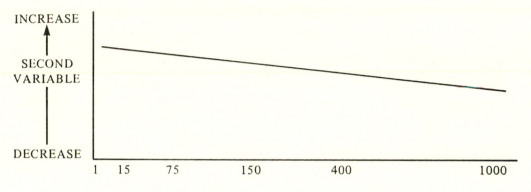

Number of officers employed by a police department.

A negative correlation exists between the number of officers employed by a police department and:

*the degree of social interaction between the
police and the community
*crime clearance rates
*personal interaction among officers

APPENDIX E

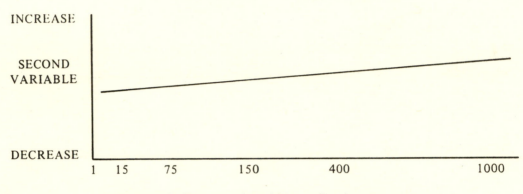

Number of officers employed by a police department.

A positive correlation exists between the number of officers employed by a police department and:

        *salary
        *formal education
        *police use of computers
        *crimes solved with computer assistance
        *formality
        *% of budget for non-salary items

APPENDIX F

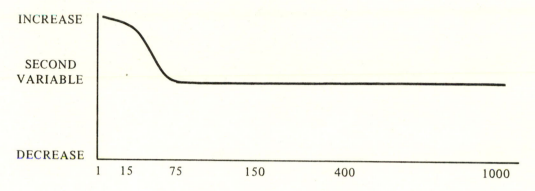

INCREASE

SECOND
VARIABLE

DECREASE

1   15   75   150   400   1000

Number of officers employed by a police department.

A correlation exists between the number of officers employed by a police department and:

> *patrol density
> *patrol deployment
> *percentage of police tax dollars spent on patrol
> *officers' feelings of loyalty to department
> *positive human relations between individual officers and citizens
> *non-criminal, non-violator, non-police incident contacts
> *group dynamics
> *self policing
> *community involvement in police arena
> *police involvement in non-police community activities
> *percent of people receiving police services

APPENDIX G

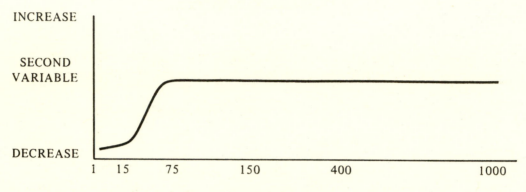

Number of officers employed by a police department.

A correlation exists between the number of officers employed by a police department and:

         *patrol costs
         *police cost to citizens
         *bureaucratic characteristics

BIBLIOGRAPHY

America's Small Town Boom. Newsweek, July 6, 1986, pp. 26-29, 32, 35, 37.

Auten, J.H. Training in the Small Department. Springfield, IL: Charles C Thomas, 1973.

Back to Basics in Crime War. U.S. News and World Report. February 17, 1986, p. 28.

Balton, M. (Ed.). European policing the Law Enforcement News interviews. New York: The John Jay Press, 1978.

Banton, M. The policeman in the community. New York: Basic Books, Inc., 1964.

Barker, B.B. Methods for reducing stress in a small police department. In Job Stress and the Police Officer — Identifying Stress Reduction Techniques — Proceedings of Symposium. Washington, DC: U.S. Government Printing Office, 1975.

Beach, R.E. The Iron Trail.

Beale, C.L. Rural and Small Town Population Change, 1970-1980. Washington, DC: U.S. Department of Agriculture, 1981.

Becker, G.S. Crime and punishment: An economic approach. Journal of Political Economy, 1968, 76, 169-217.

Bell, D.J. The police role and higher education. Journal of Police Science and Administration, 1979, 7, 467-475.

Bopp, W.J. & Schultz, D.O. A Short History of American Law Enforcement. Springfield, IL: Charles C Thomas, 1972.

Born, D.O. Crime in the country. The Country Gentleman, Fall 1981, pp. 26-31.

Breathnach, S. The Irish police. Dublin: Anvil Books Ltd., 1974.

Bristow, A.P. Rural Law Enforcement. Boston: Allyn and Bacon, Inc., 1982.

Caiden, G.E. Police revitalization. Lexington, MA: D. C. Heath, 1977.

Cain, M. Society and the policeman's role. London & Boston: Routledge & Kegan Paul Ltd., 1972.

Carlson, J.E., Lassey, M.L., & Lassey, W.R. Rural Society and Environment in America. New York: McGraw-Hill Book Company, 1981.

The Carter administration small community and rural development policy. Washington, DC: U.S. Government Printing Office, 1980.

Chapman, S.G. (Ed.) The police heritage in England and America. East Lansing: Michigan State University, 1963.

Chapman, S.G. Rural police in England and Wales. Journal of Criminal Law, Criminology, and Police Science, 1954, 45, 499-501.

Commission on Accreditation for Law Enforcement Agencies, Inc., 1984 Brochure.

Crank, P., et al. "Cynicism Among Police Chiefs," Justice Quarterly. Vol. 3, No. 3; (Sept. 1986), pp. 341-352.

Cronk, S.D. (Ed.) A Beginning Assessment of the Justice System in Rural Areas. Washington, DC: National Rural Center, 1977.

Cross, P.K. Adults as learners. San Francisco: Jossey-Bass Publishers, 1981.

Daviss, B. From Urban Sprawl to Country Drawl. Police Magazine, July 1983, p. 51-56.

Decker, S.H. Discretion and criminal justice. Beverly Hills, CA: Sage Publications, 1978.

Decker, S.H. The working personality of rural policemen. LAE Journal of the American Criminal Justice Association, 1978, 41, 19-28.

Donno, D. (Ed.) The Prince and selected discourses: Machiavelli. New York: Bantam, 1971.

Donovan, P. The Municipal Police: A Rural and Urban Comparison (Doctoral Dissertation, University of Missouri, 1971). Dissertation Abstracts International, 1971, 32, (University Microfilms No. 71-22904).

Eastman, G.D. & Eastman, E.M. (Eds.) Municipal Police Administration. Washington, DC: International City Management Association, 1971.

Felkenes, G.T. Quality of Police education. The Police Chief, September 1980, pp. 44-46.

Forced Retirement Cuts Force From 1 Police Officer - To None. The Clarion Ledger, January 5, 1981, p. 4A (Jackson, MS)

Franks, W.D. A time for change. The Police Chief, November 1978, p. 18.

Galliher, J.F., Donovan, L.P. & Adams, D.L. Small-Town Police - Trouble, Tasks, and Publics. Journal of Police Science and Administration, 1975, 3, pp. 19-28.

Gilbert, J.N. Criminal Investigation. 2nd edition. Columbus, OH: Charles E. Merrill Publishing Co., 1986.

Ginsberg, M. Rural criminal justice—an overview. American Journal of Criminal Law, 1974, 3, 35-51.

Goldstein, H. Policing a Free Society. Cambridge, MA: Ballinger Publishing Company, 1977.

Hangberg, R., Unkovic, C.M. Southern County Sheriffs - Multifaceted Law Enforcement Agents. Journal of Police Science and Administration, 1978, 6, 311-317.

Harper and Row (Producer). Rural Crime. Hagerstown, MD: Harper and Row Media Order Fulfillment, 1978. (Audiocassette/Film)

Her Majesty's Stationery Office. Police manpower, equipment and efficiency. London: Author, 1967.

Hicks, R.D. Undercover Operations and Persuasion. Springfield, Illinois: Charles C Thomas, 1973.

Hindus, M.S. Prison and plantation—criminal justice in nineteenth-century Massachusetts and South Carolina (Doctoral dissertation, University of California, Berkeley, 1975). (University Microfilms No. 76-15,219)

Hoffer, E. The Ordeal of Change.

Hubbard, R.D. & Horton, D.M. Rural Crime and Criminal Justice: A Selected Bibliography. Washington, DC: National Institute of Justice, 1980.

International Association of Chiefs of Police. Criminal justice education directory (Rev. ed.). Gaithersburg, MD. Author, 1980.

International Conference of Police Associations. Wage and benefit survey. Washington, DC: Author, 1975.

Isherwood, R. & Holt, A. Rural beat policing. Police Research Bulletin, July 1968, 7, 8-15.

Jay, A. Management and Machiavelli. New York: Bantam Books, 1969.

Johnson, H.W. Crime, delinquency and criminal justice services in rural America. Human Services in the Rural Environment, 1978, 3, 1-5.

Kenney, J.P., Pursuit, D.G., Fuller, D.E. & Barry, R.F. Police Work with Juveniles and the Administration of Juvenile Justice. Springfield, IL: Charles C Thomas, 1982.

Koepsell, T.W. & Girard, C.M. Small police agency consolidation: Suggested approaches. Washington, DC: U.S. Government Printing Office, 1979.

Law Enforcement Assistance Administration. Two hundred years of American criminal justice. Washington, DC: U.S. Government Printing Office, 1976.

Leonard, V.A. Central Police University. The Police Chief, September 1980, pp. 44-46.

Leuci, B. Lecture, University of Southern Mississippi, February 16, 1982.

Manning, P.K. & Van Maanen, J., Eds. Policing: A View From the Street. Santa Monica, CA: Goodyear Publishing Company, 1978.

MGM home video. The Long Riders.

McClure, J. Cop World. New York: Dell Publishing Company, Inc., 1984.

McGinnis, W.H. Small Department Work Schedule. The Police Chief, July 1974, pp. 61-62.

Medeiros, K.H. Small Police Departments Committee Report. The Police Chief, March 1985, p. 146.

Monroe, D.G. & Garrett, E.W. Police conditions in the United States. Montclair, NJ: Patterson Smith, 1968.

Morris, W.R. The Twelfth of August. New York: Bantam Books, Inc., 1974.

National Advisory Commission on Criminal Justice Standards and Goals. Report on Police. Washington, DC: United States Government Printing Office, 1973.

National Commission on Law Observance and Enforcement. Report on police. Washington, DC: U.S. Government Printing Office, 1931. No. 14.

National Sheriffs' Association. County law enforcement—an assessment of capabilities and needs. Washington, DC: U.S. Department of Justice Law Enforcement Assistance Administration, 1978.

Nelson, R. The Cop Who Wouldn't Quit. New York: Bantam Books, Inc., 1984.

Niederhoffer, A. & Blumberg, A.S. The ambivalent force: Perspectives on the police. San Francisco, CA: Rinehart Press, 1973.

Ostrom, E. & Parks, R.B. Suburban police departments: Too many and too small? In L.H. Masotti & J.K. Hadden (Eds.), The Urbanization of the Suburbs (Vol. 7). Los Angeles: Sage Publications, Inc., 1973.

Ostrom, E., Parks, R.B. & Whitaker, G.P. Police agency size: Some evidence of its effects. Police Studies, 1978, 1(1), 34-46.

Ostrom, E. & Whitaker, G.P. Patterns of Metropolitan Policing. Cambridge, MA. Ballinger Publishing Co., 1978.

Ostrom, E., Parks, R.B., & Whitaker, G.P. Policing metropolitan America. Washington, DC: National Science Foundation, 1977.

Palazzolo, C.S. Small Groups. New York: D. Van Nostrand Company, 1981.

Parker, A.E. The Berkeley Police Story, Springfield, IL: Charles C Thomas, 1972.

Patel, D.I. Exurbs: Urban Residential Development in the Countryside. Washington, DC: University Press of America, Inc., 1980.

Pirsig, R.M. Zen and the Art of Motorcycle Maintenance. New York: Bantam Books, Inc., 1974.

President's Commission on Law Enforcement and Administration of Justice. The Challenge of Crime in a Free Society. Washington, DC: U.S. Government Printing Office, 1967.

Radelet, L.A. The Police and the Community. Encino, CA: Glencoe Publishing Co., Inc., 1973.

Ridgeway, C. The Dynamics of Small Groups. New York: St. Martin's Press, 1983.

Rosenberg, H. 'Dukes' is 'eat up' with potentially dangerous grammar. The Clarion Ledger, April 23, 1982, p. 8D. (Jackson, MS)

Ruff, H.J. How to prosper during the coming bad years. New York: Warner Books, 1981.

Sandy, J.P. & Devine, D.A. Four stress factors unique to rural patrol. The Police Chief, September 1978, pp. 42-44.

Saunders, C.B., Jr. Upgrading the American police. Washington, DC: The Brookings Institution, 1970.

Sergiovanni, T.J. & Starratat, R.J. Supervision: Human Perspectives. New York: McGraw-Hill Book Company, 1979.

Shepherd, C.R. Small Groups: Some Sociological Perspectives. San Francisco: Chandler, 1964.

Sherman, L.W. The quality of police education. San Francisco: Jossey-Bass Publishers, 1978.

Sims, V.H. Education, Training, Age, Salaries, and Military Experience of Local Police Officers by Size of Agency in Mississippi (Doctoral Dissertation, University of Southern Mississippi, 1982). Dissertation Abstracts International, 1983, 44, (University Microfilms No. 83-11079).

Sims, V.H. Manpower Characteristics of Arizona's Small Police Departments (Masters theses, Arizona State University, 1975).

Sims, V.H. Rural and Small Town Police. The Police Chief, July 1982, p. 29.

Sims, V.H. Rural Police Internship Program Works. Law and Order, October 1981, p. 58.

Skolnick, J.H. & Bayley, D.H. The New Blue Line. New York: The Free Press, 1986.

Smith, B. Rural crime control. New York: Institute of Public Administration, Columbia University, 1933.

Stratton, J.G. Police Passages. Manhattan Beach, CA: Glennon Publishing Company, 1984.

Taft, P.B. Keeping the Peace in the New Wild West. Police Magazine. July 1981, pp. 8-17.

Teske, R.H.C. Small Town and University Policing. The Police Chief, February 1982, p. 44.

Toews, Baker, Thompson & Schapiro. Rural poverty and rural justice. A Beginning Assessment of the Justice System in Rural Areas. Washington, DC: National Rural Center, 1977.

U.S. Department of Justice, Federal Bureau of Investigation. Crime in the United States. Washington, DC: U.S. Government Printing Office, 1980.

U.S. Department of Justice, Law Enforcement Assistance Administration. Sourcebook of Criminal Justice Statistics 1977. Washington, DC: U.S. Government Printing Office, 1978.

U.S. Department of Justice, Law Enforcement Assistance Administration. Sourcebook of Criminal Justice Statistics 1981. Washington, DC: U.S. Government Printing Office, 1982.

Velikovsky, I. Mankind in amnesia. Garden City, NY: Doubleday & Company, 1982.

Vollmer, A. The police and modern society. Montclair, NJ: Patterson Smith, 1971. (Originally copyrighted, 1936).

Walker, S. A critical history of police reform. Lexington, MA: D.C. Heath and Company, 1977.

Walker, S. The police in America. New York: McGraw-Hill, 1983.

Ward, S.M. Rural crime and law enforcement: A perspective. A Beginning Assessment of the Justice System in Rural Areas. Washington, DC: National Rural Center, 1977.

Wasby, S.L. Small town police and the Supreme Court. Lexington, MA: D.C. Heath and Company, 1976.

Whitehead, D. Attack on terror: The FBI against the ku klux klan in Mississippi. New York: Funk & Wagnalls, 1970.

Wisdom, G.A. & Bennett, J.W. The rural peace officer. The Police Chief, March 1979, pp. 36-37.

Zapke, R.A. Police management guidelines for rural communities. Rockville, MD: National Criminal Justice Research Service, Manual No. NCJ-34496.

INDEX